DIGGING THROUGH

A Guide to Biblical Discovery

BY

STEVEN PAUL JOHNSON

MAR 2:4 MKJV

(4) WHEN THEY COULD NOT COME NEAR TO HIM BECAUSE OF THE CROWD, THEY UNROOFED THE ROOF WHERE HE WAS. AND DIGGING THROUGH, THEY LET DOWN THE COT ON WHICH THE PARALYTIC WAS LYING.

Cover Artwork by Kip Ayers Illustration
(http://www.kipayersillustration.com)

ISBN: 1470085593
ISBN 13: 9781470085599

TABLE OF CONTENTS

FOREWORD

The market for "How to Study the Bible" books is large and growing. Every Christian bookstore is filled with study aids and new tools for teaching us how to study the Bible. Some are good and useful at helping us to learn to use our Bibles and become more aware of the "letter" of the Word. But often what we want is best obtained by pursing something else. It's the fruit, not actually the goal. I believe that to be the case with the whole how to study the Bible process. We discover the most, not when we study the Bible, but when we pursue Him.

Believers often miss the real benefit of the Good News and continue to live with poverty of soul. A place of deficiency should never exist in us who profess to love the Word as long as we discover that the Word is a revelation of Jesus and when we study the Word, the Word studies us.

God is rising up healthy fathers (and mothers) who know the Father God and will help us all find our true identity as we receive a revelation of Jesus. These Fathers have been changed by God and excite me to no end for they do not teach for you to learn something, but they teach for you to discover someone. This allows sons and daughters to not live with an intellectual awareness of Jesus but by the Spirit, to be led into a revelation of Him that allows us to have our hearts anchored in a world we cannot see. It's a place where we realize He was not hiding from us but for us and He loves it when we pursue and discover Him in a way that leads to transformation, not just more information. This is where Steve Johnson and his wonderful book, Digging Through, come into play. Steve is a true spiritual father. He speaks to us as family gathered around the Christmas tree. Generously he gives away to each of us incredibly valuable gifts of tools to discover Jesus, and through that encounter with the living Word, to be transformed.

This is the best book I have ever read on this subject matter. The pages are rich in Kingdom principles and revelation that anchors the reader into a biblical perspective on life that has largely been missing in books of this type. Digging Through is rich in insight and filled with exciting potential, all the while liberating the heart to dream bigger and bolder. This book is an invitation to encounter the Father of life. Come join the journey and begin to experience the Word come alive! You will never be the same!

Stan Tyra
Sr. Leader, Revolution Church
Rogers, Arkansas

INTRODUCTION

M en are fools for rules. We love guidelines, rules of thumb, and regulations because ultimately, these provide us with some security – in whatever. I recall riding with my grandmother back in my teen years. She loved to take trips and more often than not, she would drive. More than once, I'd be sitting either in the front seat or the back… telephone poles whizzing by in such a way that resembled when Han Solo would kick the Millennium Falcon into hyper-drive. I'm sorry if the reference is lost on you. It was FAST. Typically, somewhere in a break of conversation, she would look down at the speedometer and say, "Oh gosh! I'm going eighty-five!" That was back when fifty-five was the speed limit on the interstate. She would let off the gas and we would get back down to fifty-five and color would begin to return to my face. Rules can provide comfort.

When a church gets crowded, inevitably a wizened, demographically astute person will approach the pastor with a remark like this: "When we hit 80%, we're full!" Why is that? Because there is generally a limit to what men will sit through in order to be fed, entertained, or informed by other men. True! But tell that to those who were trying to get close to Jesus in Mark 2:4.

<hr>

MAR 2:4 MKJV

> (4) When they could not come near to Him because of the crowd, they unroofed the roof where He was. And digging through, they let down the cot on which the paralytic was lying.

The house was full – beyond full – and the fire marshal would have shut the place down had he known. But these men had a goal of reaching Jesus, and reach Him they did, even if it meant going in through the roof! They had a paralyzed friend and they needed a solution that the world was not offering. They needed an encounter with the Living Word.

For many of us, studying scripture is paralyzing. There's no place to start! The answer is simple, really. Pick a spot. If you really believe Jesus is on the inside, then start slinging that pickaxe because you will find Him! It takes work and some endurance, but the end result will be breakthrough! Breakthrough is the goal. Like so many worthwhile endeavors, studying the Bible can be slow-going and somewhat tedious. Much like playing an instrument, when you finally learn to play a song, you must be happy and content to know that song! Otherwise, frustration tries to set in because you've only scratched the surface of what appears to be a universe full of songs to learn. On the outset, let me encourage you to be content that you are growing in the Word. Jesus had many relationships on earth – and all were different. He knew Peter, but not like He knew John the Baptist. He knew the Samaritan woman at the well, but not in the same way He knew Nicodemus. He loved everyone, and everyone got all of Jesus that they were willing to pursue. This is our choice, too.

This book will provide some elements which may seem quite fundamental to many of you who have been on your Christian walk for quite a long time. However, with every topic my intent is to provide an adequate foundation for anyone who may be new to digging in the Word. To give you some security, I want to outline some rules for studying scripture. Additionally, I incorporated some discoveries (nuggets) that I thought to be profound – at any level of scholarship. It's my belief that once a person realizes the depth of the Word and the number of treasures buried there, they might be incurably hooked to the process of digging those treasures out! So I certainly hope that there is something in this book that can help you grow spiritually, even if your last name is Graham!

Why does anybody study? What is the draw? Before I go any further, I should at least expound upon my own beliefs regarding the

Bible so that you will have insight as to why I've chosen the study methods I have. My desire is to impart to you more than methodology for study. Chances are, what works for me will not be so effective for most of you. However, the methods here are valid and worthy of exploration and experimentation. Far beyond method, I would like to share insight on *how to think* when reading scripture. Recognition of suspicious words and phrases – things I call **hollow tiles** – can be the key to incredible revelation! I would also like to say that you cannot read or study your way into a relationship with God. This sets Christianity apart from other religions of the world. The basic premise of Christianity is that it requires a child-like faith to receive the reward it offers, rather than years of toiling to achieve a type of intellectual enlightenment. It's not about how much you know! It is, however, about your desire to seek Him, and His word is a great place to start!

DOES THE BIBLE HAVE ERRORS?

I believe the Bible is God's word – inerrant – and true from cover to cover. I even believe my name on the cover, Steve Johnson. I believe that. Timothy said it best, however:

2TI 3:16-17 MKJV

(16) All Scripture is God-breathed, and is profitable for doctrine, for reproof, for correction, for instruction in righteousness,

(17) that the man of God may be perfected, thoroughly furnished to every good work.

To point out the very first hollow tile of this book, anything God-breathed is LIVING. We first see God breathing in Genesis 2:7 when He created Adam from dust and "breathed into his nostrils the breath of life; and man became a living soul." To have God's breath is to have something eternal – something that cannot be destroyed! Have you ever wondered at all the failed attempts to destroy Bibles? There! Right off the bat I have started throwing scriptures at you. Please realize that there is no substitute for experience. If you've never read through the bible or memorized a verse, then there won't be many scriptures that just pop into your head. Once you have read the Bible through once or twice, however, you will notice that stories and passages start coming to mind much more often. Don't be discouraged if none of these references seem familiar! I do hope you will open your Bible and re-read these passages that intrigue you.

God breathed His word into the hearts of those who penned it. It was written by approximately forty men over the course of 1500 years. This, in itself, turns many people off. They want to know that the information they are ingesting is valid, being unable to comprehend a work authored by so many people over more than a millennium – especially if the work is laying a claim such as being the WORD of GOD. The truth of the matter is that most people who wish to understand the Bible find that much of it is incomprehensible. Why? Because it is a direct reflection of its author, God Himself! I am not making excuses for my own inability to explain certain teachings within the book. My goal is to teach you how to approach Bible study without revealing every mystery you may encounter (as if I could). God is bigger than all of us, and very mysterious. What you will find as you read and study, however, is that God hides things for you, not from you. An analogy my spiritual mentor likes to use is to suppose a grandfather had hidden some candy for his grandchildren. Would he hide it in such a way that his grandbabies couldn't find it? No! In fact, if he didn't think it could be found where it was currently hidden, he would move it to a place where he knew it could be found! This is how I believe God teaches us, too. This changes everything!

Yes, I believe the Bible is inerrant. I believe God is so big and so powerful that He has absolutely maintained the integrity of His own word. What a concept! I realize that this offends the intellect of most people, and for you, please reason with me for a few pages. From the beginning of time the devil has tried to destroy this Word, but he has failed in every attempt. There have been Bible burnings, false translations, additions, subtractions... you name it

– it has been tried. Yet the Word is still the Word – it's still available, widely, and in all different types of languages. It's still a best seller for goodness sake! The Gospel is still the Gospel in all its glory.

But what about all the changes? Again, does God have the power and desire to preserve His instruction to us, or not? Many opponents of the idea that God authored the Bible start from the pretense that man has changed the word many times over, rendering it unrecognizable from its original form. The problem with this idea is that it supposes God to be uncaring about protecting His word. It supposes God to be impotent to protect what He said, and it supposes US to be so smart as to pull the wool over the eyes of millions. *The true scholar of the Word* will find that the precepts that are in our written Word are so brilliant that they are absolutely beyond any human ability to perceive, and all attempts to explain these precepts from a human point of view are truly silly. The Bible IS the signature of the Holy Spirit – and this cannot be forged by man (see the chapter on Hidden Levels of Understanding). Although the purpose of this book is not to convince you that the scriptures are inerrant, I do invite you to keep reading because I believe that many of the topics we cover will create questions as to mans' ability to write such a book as the Bible!

THE BIBLE IS FOR TODAY, AND TOMORROW

The Bible is a prophetic book. Although scholars do not agree on the exact number of prophecies contained in scripture, it's not difficult to find over 10,000, many of them already having been fulfilled. Why would that be? Why would God place such an emphasis upon the future? When we begin to see the heart of God through His Word, we soon discover that He does not dwell nearly so much upon who you are as who you will be! He has plans for you (Jeremiah 29:11). God's desire is to reveal Himself through His Word and in so doing, reveal who you are to Him. It is with this realization that we begin to see His plans for us. That is why the book is prophetic in nature.

This is the foundation of where we will start our book. How do we study the Word of God? Is there an art to digging? How do we study God Himself? It is my hope that by reading this book, you will begin to see that scripture really is the signature of the Holy Spirit and that you will begin a new, intimate walk with the Author! Read on!

WHY ARE YOU STUDYING?

We all study the Bible for different reasons. One who writes a book report will likely study differently than one who is studying in order to become closer to the book's author. There are style studies, word studies, and contextual studies. It could be a verse at a time, a chapter, a book, or a thesis on the entire Word. Back to the idea that grandfather is hiding candy from us. Granted, I do not know your grandfather. If he is spiteful, then turning over all the living room furniture in order to find a jolly rancher is probably not worth it. But if I believe that grandpa means for me to have some candy, and that we may be talking chocolate, then I search with vigor. Our reason for studying will dictate our method.

Early in my life, I studied the word because I was challenged to do so. There were other smart kids in Sunday school who I personally wished to show up. Being the fastest at the sword drill (finding a specific book of the Bible as fast as possible) had its merit, even if only for 45 minutes a week. I wanted to know the human author of each book. I wanted to know the time period in which it was written. All this – because I wanted someone to be impressed that I knew it. I would be the last to say that this motivation has no credence. After all, this knowledge has served me well throughout my life. But after a while, learning for this reason grew old and I never really got a girlfriend because of it. Additionally, there are very few adults who have the time or interest to sit at home and memorize the books of the Bible for the sake of being the fastest gun in Sunday school. In fact, I would venture to say that most people who ask me the question of how to study have one goal in mind: How can I learn more about the God I serve?

As believers, we are admonished to study God's word.

2TI 2:15 MKJV

(15) Study earnestly to present yourself approved to God, a workman that does not need to be ashamed, rightly dividing the Word of Truth.

Let us be careful that we do not take this verse the wrong way. We who are in Jesus are righteous before God, but to be a workman carries a measure of responsibility. Those who are called to teach (all of us to a certain extent) also have the responsibility to teach Truth with great care not to mislead. We must *rightly divide* His Word. The implication is obvious. One can wrongly divide the Word, which we will discuss in a later chapter. The other possibility as I see it is that some will present themselves before God in an 'unapproved' way. I don't even know what this means, but it sounds unpleasant!

It is established that your belief of who God is and what the Bible is WILL dictate how you study. Because I believe God is the supernatural author and that every word of the Bible is inspired and true, I read scriptures with a suspicious eye. I know in my heart that every word was placed purposefully, and that every sentence was phrased carefully to reveal or conceal a mystery. On the other hand, if I approached my study from the angle that this was a compiled document, crafted by the hand of man and changed multiple times over the eons, then my method will probably reflect this – never reaching the point of forensic investigation because honestly, what would be the purpose?

I have felt for many years that part of my purpose in life was to introduce Christians to Jesus. I realize that is an odd thing to say! Yet, most of us who know a few good Christian folks will acknowledge that – to my frustration – they don't always act very Christ-like. They get bogged down on worldly affairs. They become distraught at the news. Depression is common. Defeated Christians are everywhere! It's disturbing! My discovery has been that very few Christians who find themselves in these ruts actually know what the Bible says about *them,* nor do they realize what the Bible (being a prophetic book) says about how everything turns out! For me, my motive for studying is to enable me to kindle a real fire in the hearts of people that have only a few embers left. Christians, if anyone, should have a great outlook on life (and death). Learning to think differently is the key!

PERSPECTIVE MATTERS

Whenever I go to the dentist for any type of repair on my teeth, I ask for nitrous oxide. Good ole' laughing gas! I will pay extra for it if I have to. For one, it really relaxes me. I can sit in the chair and within just a few moments, I feel as though I am falling through the chair! It's not a bad thing... but it is a DIFFERENT thing! Then I begin to think of things I never think of in my normal state of mind. Yeah, yeah, I know. It's getting high and I'm fully aware of that. But I think of things while in that chair that – if I had a notepad – I would write down because I know they are totally outside the realm of my normal thought process. I want to save them to read later! Alas, I have never done this. I'm still curious as to whether or not they would actually make sense if I were to read them with a clear head. But my point is this: thinking in a different way can be so liberating! Sometimes perspective is everything! A different perspective on an unpleasant issue may relieve much pain! For this reason it is very important to receive Godly counsel when going through personal trials. Godly counsel will always provide hope amidst the storm because God's perspective is likely to be different than our own, especially when the clouds are dark. We will discuss this more later.

But the scriptures are not only life to Christians… they are life to everyone! John chapter one says that Jesus is the Living Word. He is the scriptures wearing a pair of sandals. Yet many of the people He came into contact with daily knew nothing of Him or His message. Still, He gave them life. He gave them hope and healing. He gave them direction. He left laughter in His wake! This is what scripture can do for a world that has very little to laugh at. Matthew 5:44 tells us to love our enemies and pray for those who persecute us. This is unconditional love of scripture! This is the heart of God for everyone! This is how everyone can be blessed by God's Word – even when they have no idea why they are blessed! It is Love without an agenda. Unfortunately, many of us who proclaim to follow the teachings of Jesus tend to attach our agendas to His message. This perversion of purpose has been prevalent for such a long time that now the world has grown paranoid and critical of anything that might be construed as 'religious'.

Another basic tenet of Christianity is that there is life after death for those who accept and believe what Jesus taught: that He is the Son of God, the Way, the Truth, and the Life (John 14:6). This presents another reason for a believer to read and study the scriptures. Imagine, if you will, that you are walking along in heaven and the prophet Ezekiel walks up to you. At introduction, he says, "Hello, I'm Ezekiel. Did you read my book?" The thought of stammering, "N… no…" to a man like him simply terrifies me! Read his book!

Seriously though, when we begin to see life through the lens of scripture, then we begin to see life as God sees it. Watching the news is depressing – if we have no hope. The plight of society and the decay of morality is a real downer – if we have no hope. In Jesus' day, things were not much different. A king could declare the destruction of all male babies between the age of birth and three. Can you imagine living under that kind of regime? Terror takes on new meaning! Caesar could decree the burning of your entire city, crucifying every inhabitant simply because 'someone' had the audacity to protest him. It happened more than once! But through scriptures we learn the mind of God, which says there is a plan! Redemption is coming! No, we are not always spared hardships, but God has a plan to change things – and He is doing it! Scriptures reveal this plan to us, and we can then take a look at the news and think, "It will be okay."

The name of this book is Digging Through. The title of this chapter could easily be... Why Dig? It's a good question, because it implies a truth. As I mentioned in the Foreword, God likes to hide things *for* us.

DEU 8:7-9 MKJV

> (7) For Jehovah your God brings you into a good land, a land of brooks of water, of fountains and depths that spring out of valleys and hills,

> (8) a land of wheat and barley and vines and fig trees and pomegranates, a land of olive oil and honey,

> (9) a land in which you shall eat bread without want. You shall not lack any thing in it. It is a land whose stones are iron, and out of whose hills you may dig copper.

Moses was describing the Promised Land to Israel. He described a land where all that was needed was readily available. Water flowed by your doorstep and grapes grew in your garden. But there were also things for which you had to dig. The Promised Land today is a place where you have everything you need, but you must dig for the extras that you *want*. The Word of God is this way. It does not take a brain surgeon to extract the Gospel. John 3:16 spells it out very clearly. The beauty of the design of scripture is that a child might read, understand, and accept. But for those who want real wealth... real abundance... there is this option to dig. Have you noticed that the gems and precious metals in the world are concealed in the darkness of the earth? Some people make their living by simply buying real estate on a mere hunch that their newly purchased plot might conceal vast riches. Nearly all who do this do so because there is a thrill involved to uncovering something hidden. Many could choose an easier way to earn a living, but they will not because revealing the concealed is addictive! So, too, is digging the gold out of scriptures.

MAT 13:44 MKJV

> (44) Again, the kingdom of Heaven is like treasure hidden in a field, which when a man has found it, he hides it, and for the joy of it goes and sells all that he has, and buys that field.

Jesus told this story to point out that the Kingdom of Heaven is this way. God Himself is this way, and therefore His Word is this way!

IT'S SO MUCH WORK!

When the bread fell from heaven to the hungry Israelites, the first thing they said was, "What is it?" In fact, that is what manna means. What is it? Jesus told the crowd:

JOH 6:32 MKJV

> (32) Then Jesus said to them, Truly, truly, I say to you, Moses did not give you that bread from Heaven, but My Father gives you the true bread from Heaven.

Just think about that for a second. Jesus has explained a mystery. He was the Bread from Heaven! Yet, by definition, they didn't understand Him. They didn't get manna, and they didn't get Jesus. After His teaching, the best they could muster was, "What is it?" You might think it got easier for his closest followers, but this really wasn't the case.

JOH 6:58-60 MKJV

(58) This is the Bread which came down from Heaven, not as your fathers ate the manna, and died; he who partakes of this Bread shall live forever.

(59) He said these things in the synagogue as He taught in Capernaum.

(60) Then when they had heard, many of His disciples said, This is a hard saying, who can hear it?

The point is that digging isn't always easy. One must get past many offenses of the mind in order to 'break through' to where Jesus is waiting to heal you. This can be a lot of sweaty, dirty work, and you may need to have some help to accomplish it.

DIGGING FOR BREAKTHROUGH

Oh, but there might come a time when you NEED to dig. The Promised Land, as we described above, was not a place without its dangers. If you will recall, it was first inhabited by giants. What would happen if such an enemy loomed on the horizon? Could you try to defend yourself using a fig? The iron you need lies just beneath the surface. The gold you need to pay your debt is just a few pick-axe swings away! When the sky is brass and there are no rain clouds on the radar, you must know that digging a well will bring you to the water of the very last downpour! Yes, right now that refreshing water you need in your parched life lies below your feet. Is it a foot beneath? Is it fifty feet down?

In Bible times, the beast of burden was the ox. The ox was yoked to a grinding wheel or a plow and he would do all the heavy hauling. Like oxen, we take on a heavy yoke from time to time that we have no idea how to remove. This yoke might be a relationship (by definition, a yoke is a **pair** of oxen), a task we are faced with, or a circumstance we are in. According to the Law of Moses, one was not to muzzle their ox while it was treading grain (Deut 25:4).

The idea was that the worker deserved to be paid! The result was that as the ox ate and ate, his neck would swell and pretty soon, the yoke would no longer fit! Either that or it would break off altogether! This is one reason we dig through scriptures in search of a breakthrough. The Word of God is bread. The more we consume, the fewer yokes are likely to fit us! Consuming the Word helps us in our realization of who we are to God, and who He is to us. Dig!

WHAT MOVES YOU?

In my quiet time recently, the Holy Spirit prompted me with the question: What moves you in your spirit? That's a funny thing to ask me, God! After all, YOU move me! But God understands – and wants me to understand – that not everything He does is geared towards me. I'm the father of twin girls. They look the same, but they are completely different. There are times when I'm interacting with them that I will do something to draw a reaction from one, knowing that it will have no effect on the other. I know what moves them! God knows what moves me and He wants me to know that He knows in order to expand my own awareness of Him! If I see someone who is sobbing in the floor during a worship service, I need to know that they were moved and that what they were moved by was REAL, even if very little has resonated within my own spirit! God may even use this realization to move me! What moves you? It's an important question!

In particular, what moves you about the Word? After all, it's easy to be moved by the story of the Roman centurion (Matthew 8:5-10) with the paralyzed son. This is an amazing story! It is full of emotion and passion. It's a story that makes most of us just sigh and meditate. Even the questions this story raises are intriguing! Let's take a quick look.

MAT 8:5-10 MKJV

(5) And when Jesus had entered into Capernaum, a centurion came to him, beseeching Him,

(6) and saying, Lord, my son lies at home paralyzed and grievously tormented.

(7) And Jesus says to him, I will come and heal him.

(8) The centurion answered and said, Lord, I am not worthy that You should come under my roof; but only speak the word, and my boy will be healed.

(9) For I am a man under authority, having soldiers under me. And I say to this one, Go! And he goes; and to another, Come! And he comes; and to my servant, Do this! And he does it.

(10) When Jesus heard, He marveled and said to those who followed, Truly I say to you, I have not found such great faith, no, not in Israel.

I'm sighing. Why does this story move me so deeply? For starters, the event moved Jesus! The text says that Jesus 'marveled' at the faith of the centurion. I do, too! Think of this: this man is a Roman. Romans, for the most part, were the ones in authority! They occupied and controlled Israel during Jesus' day. But nothing humbles us more than our human condition. This man was the father of a sick boy. Can you feel his desperation? What would it take for a Roman officer to beg help from a strange Jewish man – a conquered subject, no less?

I told you this story raised questions for me. Did it for you? What are your questions? Think about them for a minute and write them down. Even if you don't believe this to be a true story, what might your questions be? If you are studying this story from a purely intellectual angle, you might end up with the conclusion that it is what it is. Jesus was compassionate. He felt like a good healing that day. He wanted to make a good impression with the Roman authorities. It's a feel-good story because it has a twist and a happy ending.

For me, there is more to it than that. To begin with, I'm impressed that Jesus is impressed. Jesus, God in the flesh, marvels at the faith of a Roman – a non-Jew. Wow! That moves me! Oh, but now my questions. Jesus said, "I will come and heal him." The centurion told Jesus that He should not have to do so, and Jesus marveled at this saying "Go. As you have said, let it be to you. And his boy was healed in that hour" (verse 13). What difference did the faith of the centurion make? What difference did his *honor* to Jesus make? Either way, Jesus was going to heal his son. Did his faith save him a few hours? Would a lack of faith have caused Jesus a long, arduous journey to the man's house? If Jesus knew He could just say the word, why didn't He opt for that at the beginning? *What – exactly – transpired here?*

Perhaps Jesus was making a point. Did you detect a shift when the faith and honor of the centurion was displayed? After I explain what happened, re-read the story and try to detect the shift. If Jesus touches you with the intent to heal, you will be healed. We can prove that by simply reading a little further in the chapter about the account of Peter's mother-in-law being healed.

MAT 8:15 MKJV

> (15) And He touched her hand, and the fever left her. And she arose and served them.

This is exactly what was going to happen to the centurion's son. However! A different element arose in the case of the centurion. His own *faith* was demonstrated through his honor of Jesus! It was the centurion's faith in Jesus that healed his son, not the physical

11

hand of Jesus. Really – is this true? Is there any way we can lend credence to this concept?

To start, I went to my trusty Bible software and did a search on 'faith' – particularly – the phrase 'your faith', and immediately I'm presented with the account of the woman with the issue of blood. Perhaps you recall this story from Sunday school. She had been bleeding for years, rendering her unclean to her Hebrew contemporaries. She took a risk of risks and touched the hem of Jesus' cloak. When she was instantly healed, what did Jesus tell her? "I healed you!" No! He said, "Your faith has saved you."

MAT 9:22 MKJV

(22) But turning and seeing her, Jesus said, Daughter, be comforted; your faith has saved you. And the woman was saved from that hour.

Wow! Okay, so let's review this precept. I can be healed by the hand of Jesus, and I can be healed by my faith in Jesus. Is one example enough to prove the point? Again, I turn to my Bible software and it shows me yet another example of 'your faith'. Two blind men accost Jesus in the street asking Him for mercy. That's Hebrew for 'heal us, please!' Jesus turned to the men, and although He touches them in this case, He makes the statement, "According to your faith…"

MAT 9:29 MKJV

(29) Then He touched their eyes, saying, According to your faith let it be to you.

This is a demonstration of the *golden rule of study,* because it's the second time a precept is illustrated in order to prove our point. I will speak more on this golden rule in our next chapter.

Let's go back to our first passage. On the surface, I'm moved by the centurion. I feel his desperation. I sense his anguish. I want to see his son healed! Jesus, apparently, wanted the very same.

What a great story! But I have also learned something from asking questions. **What difference did the faith of the centurion make if his son was to be healed either way?** The Centurion acknowledged a reality that was more superior to his own, visible, reality. That reality stated that Jesus was not one of his conquered subjects, but that He was actually the one in authority. In yielding to that reality, the Centurion enabled the rules of Jesus' reality to manifest in his own life and in the lives of those in his care. The result was the immediate healing of his son. What kind of life lessons can we learn from this account?

This story moved me!

Compare this story to the genealogy of Jesus as given in Matthew 1. Go ahead – read it. Let's face it. That's dry! That's a lot o' begat'in. I can see where some names are familiar, and it's mildly interesting on the surface, at best. If you're starting out your studies in the Word and you have never read this, it certainly will not hurt you to read it. But if you find it dry, just keep reading. Don't dwell on something that doesn't move you! Read until something pops out at you.

I have given guitar lessons for a number of years. I've found that most beginning students quit for two reasons.

1. It's painful to get started. Bleeding fingers are no fun!
2. Fundamentals can be boring!

Studying the Bible is not much different at first. Relating one story to another is impossible when you have never read the book before. There is no basis to compare anything! That's not to say that reading the Bible through the first time cannot be captivating. It can! Just keep in mind that not everything is going to make sense the first (or second, or third…) time, so don't get frustrated. Keep reading! Just like a beginning guitarist, reading the Bible for the first time also seems a bit painful. After all, there is a lot of 'do this', 'do that', but 'do NOT do this or that'. Who likes reading an instruction manual? On the other hand, who likes reading a love letter written directly to you? It comes as a product of time, but you will begin to see the love by which the words were written to

13

their recipients (you, maybe?). When this happens, you will also see that the do's and don'ts are a lot less abrasive.

If you read long enough, something WILL pop out at you because the Holy Spirit is at work. He is going to get your attention if you give Him the least little opportunity. If you don't know Him, He will zap your attention when you don't see it coming. He is the author of this Word, and He desires a relationship with the reader – no matter who it is!

I have always gravitated towards the Old Testament. The stories seem more outlandish – more unbelievable! For instance, let's take a quick look at Jonathan, David's best friend. From Sunday school, we may remember just a few facts about Jonathan like: he loved David like a brother. His dad, Saul, wanted to kill David. Saul wanted Jonathan to be king and hated that Jonathan was David's friend. Yes, we know Saul had major issues, but we should also remember that in that culture at that time, an incoming king would often put to death the deposed king and his entire family! As Bible characters go, Jonathan is an amazing study. He's a guy that appears on the surface as though he would be a good vacation buddy. But Jonathan was also a man of faith and had a measure of spiritual fortitude. Let's take a look at him from this angle:

1SA 14:4-15 MKJV

> (4) And between the passages by which Jonathan sought to go over to the Philistines' garrison there was a rocky crag on the one side and a rocky crag on the other side. And the name of the one was Bozez, and the name of the other Seneh.

> (5) The one crag was a pillar on the north in front of Michmash, and the other southward in front of Gibeah.

> (6) And Jonathan said to the young man who bore his armor, Come, and let us go over to the garrison of these uncircumcised ones. It may be that Jehovah will work for

us. For there is no restraint to Jehovah, to save by many or by few.

(7) And his armor-bearer said to him, Do all that is in your heart. Turn, for behold, I am with you according to your heart.

(8) And Jonathan said, Behold, we will go over to these men, and we will show ourselves to them.

(9) If they say this to us, Stand still until we come to you, then we will stand still in our place and will not go up to them.

(10) But if they say this, Come up to us, then we will go up, for Jehovah has delivered them up into our hand. And this shall be a sign to us.

(11) And both of them showed themselves to the garrison of the Philistines. And the Philistines said, Behold, the Hebrews come out of the holes where they have hidden themselves.

(12) And the men of the garrison answered Jonathan and his armor-bearer and said, Come up to us, and we will teach you a thing. And Jonathan said to his armor-bearer, Come up after me, for Jehovah has delivered them into the hand of Israel.

(13) And Jonathan climbed up on his hands and feet, and his armor-bearer after him. And they fell before Jonathan, and his armor-bearer killed after him.

(14) And this was the first blow, when Jonathan and his armor-bearer struck about twenty men in about half of a furrow of an acre of a field.

(15) And there was trembling in the army, in the field, and among all the people. The garrison and the spoilers also trembled, and the earth quaked, and it was a very great trembling.

Now I ask in all seriousness... who could make up such a great story! One of the things I love about this story is the humor that riddles it. I find the armor bearer as captivating as Jonathan! The first thing I notice was the bold statement of faith that Jonathan declared: "Jehovah is not limited to save by many or by few." Wow! Can you imagine wearing that badge as a soldier? A mere intellectual acknowledgement of that fact would not be enough to get me to take on those kinds of odds. It would have to be heart knowledge of God's nature!

Secondly, imagine the scenery. These two guys are walking in a canyon-like area where the fortified area at the top would be an insurmountable position for any attacker. That is, unless the attackers have the faith of Jonathan and his armor bearer.

Next, the armor bearer is fascinating! Who has this kind of loyalty? "Do whatever you like Jonathan. I'm by your side." Not... "Can we devise a better plan? This is the worst idea ever, Jonathan. On strategies, this ranks in the top one or two worst all-time strategies ever conceived, dude." I find this funny because it is simply abnormal! There is a precept hidden within this story that I call "throwing the fleece".

If you read about Gideon, you discover the concept of 'throwing the fleece', or testing God in something. It works like this:

JDG 6:36-37 MKJV

(36) And Gideon said to God, If You will save Israel by my hand, as You have said,

(37) behold, I will put a fleece of wool in the grain-floor. And if the dew is on the fleece only, and dry upon all the ground, then I shall know that You will save Israel by my hand, as You have said.

One might say... wow, what a lack of faith. Yes, possibly, but in this case God honored Gideon in his lack of faith and answered his prayer by making the fleece wet with dew while the ground around it was dry. Now, from the story we also know that Gideon had to cast the fleece again (asking God for opposite results) in order to muster the courage to act. But what we learn from Gideon is that casting a fleece when we are uncertain is *sometimes* a viable method of acquiring direction from God. However, we need to pay attention to how the fleece-test worked for Gideon. The fleece had nothing to do with the question in his mind: should I step into the role of savior of Israel? Gideon could have asked God something like, "God, if you want me to save Israel, please allow the people to rally around me with a great battle cry!" This would have been a test – related to the task at hand – that would have given Gideon a greater sense of self-confidence. But it would not have been a *legal* 'fleece', because God intended Gideon to proceed in faith, not in knowledge!

Back to Jonathan and his trusty armor bearer. Notice the fleece that Jonathan cast!

1SA 14:8-10 MKJV

(8) And Jonathan said, Behold, we will go over to these men, and we will show ourselves to them.

(9) If they say this to us, Stand still until we come to you, then we will stand still in our place and will not go up to them.

(10) But if they say this, Come up to us, then we will go up, for Jehovah has delivered them up into our hand. And this shall be a sign to us.

Jonathan's litmus test for victory was *horrible*! When the enemy sees us, if they say "wait and we'll come to you", then we will stand our ground. But if they say, "Hey come attack us on our fortified position, morons!" then we know that God has delivered them into

17

our hand. Again... this is the worst strategy EVER! But Jonathan saw this 'fleece' as a sure-fire way to know God's will in that situation and he was right!

Oh, and to make it even funnier, Jonathan says, "*Come up after me, for Jehovah has delivered them into the hand of Israel.*" Yep, Yohan, you and me... we are Israel! That slays me. And speaking of slaying, the story says that they fell before Jonathan, and his armor bearer killed after him! Readers, if you can find a friend like this, hang on to them for dear life! This story MOVES me!

PROMISES OF GOD

But it isn't necessarily the stories that move me about scripture. Sometimes it is the promises God made that make my eyes water.

MAL 3:16-18 MKJV

(16) Then those fearing Jehovah spoke together, each man to his neighbor. And Jehovah listened and heard. And a book of remembrance was written before Him for those who feared Jehovah, and for those esteeming His name.

(17) And they shall be Mine, says Jehovah of Hosts, for the day that I will make up My treasure. And I will pity them as a man has pity on his son who serves him.

(18) Then you shall again see the difference between the righteous and the wicked, between him who serves God, and him who does not serve Him.

This passage speaks to me so deeply that it is difficult for me to expound on it. When the pastor that officiated my wedding to Darci asked us for a scripture on which to base our union, we gave him this passage. God listens to us. He cares about what we care about, and He takes a special pride in those who fear Him and who speak to one another about Him. Then He says this incredible thing: "And they shall be Mine". This is God, the Creator of the universe laying claim to specific people – not huge people groups – and writing their names in His book! It's an intimate, personal thing. He calls them His *treasure*. Would you attempt to lay your hands on anything God was protecting as His treasure? Then He says in a somewhat menacing way, "you shall see the difference between the righteous and the wicked, between him who serves God, and him who does not serve Him." What that does to my spirit! It endears me to God as my Father who is jealous over me. It makes me feel not only treasured, but safe. It's not a story, but it is a promise and it moves me tremendously!

THE GOLDEN RULE

At this point, it would be a good time to share with you a golden rule of study. As we saw in the previous chapter, if we arrive at a precept through study that we believe will turn into something that we might be dogmatic about, I need to find examples in multiple places in scripture. Why? Because God Himself announced His own golden rule for establishing anything:

DEU 19:15B MKJV

(15) One witness shall not rise up against a man for any iniquity, or for any sin, in any sin that he sins. At the mouth of two witnesses, or at the mouth of three witnesses, shall the matter be made sure.

God is saying here that anything worth being dogmatic about will be taught or demonstrated multiple times. Have you ever wondered what the Bible might say if you totally ripped out the Book of John? It would say the same thing (although with less resolution) because the gospel that we find in John is repeated in the books of Matthew, Mark, and Luke. But it even gets more granular than that! Let's take a look at John chapter 1:

JOH 1:1-2 MKJV

(1) In the beginning was the Word, and the Word was with God, and the Word was God.

(2) He was in the beginning with God.

Let's assume that I'm familiar with the concept that Jesus is the "Word" (John 1:14), and I'm about to teach a Sunday school class about Jesus being present at the beginning of time. What a great topic! This passage seems fairly clear. He, Jesus, *was* in the beginning with God. Additionally, scripture goes on to say:

JOH 1:3 MKJV

(3) All things came into being through Him, and without Him not even one thing came into being that has come into being.

This is clearly communicated – perhaps beyond question – but for the purpose of our example we will explore a little further. In order to satisfy our golden rule, we need another testimony from within scripture to insure that this is an 'established' concept that we can be dogmatic about.

Granted, John again verifies this, if not years later and in a different writing:

1JN 1:1 MKJV

(1) That which was from the beginning, which we have heard, which we have seen with our eyes, which we have looked upon, and our hands have handled, concerning the Word of Life,

To some, this might not be good enough, as John cannot testify to the validity of his own statement! But it is of interest that John began both of his writings with the same message! Let's see if someone else will bear witness with John that Jesus was 'in the beginning'. Moses wrote:

GEN 1:1 MKJV

(1) In the beginning God created the heavens and the earth.

This, in itself, doesn't appear to help much. What we need to know about this is the word for 'God' that is used is 'Elohim', which is a plural Hebrew word! Interesting! Why would it be plural? Perhaps this is because God the Father was present with Spirit and *Son*? Proof.... Maybe not. But it is definitely a hint! Yes, but... How did I KNOW that? After all, this book is supposed to teach us how to figure stuff like that out! Now might be a good time to state that there is no shortcut to studying scriptures. It takes work. It takes time! The wonderful thing about study, however, is that it always pays off if you stay with it – not unlike digging for gold. The more you dig, the more you find. The more you find, the more you realize that everything is connected. There are oodles of patterns and ideals that repeat and these are what come to mind when you stick with it! Keep in mind, also, that if you do not dig, then you are limited to what you are given. That's fine, unless you are given fool's gold. You never really know unless you are able to verify truth for yourself!

So what if Jesus was present at the beginning of Creation? Does it stop there? Are there any other instances that might suggest such a thing? Funny you should ask! In the book of Judges in chapter 13, a man named Manoah (the father of Samson) was visited by an angel. Oh! But strangely... the word Angel is capitalized! That's a strange occurrence. Not realizing whom (or what) he was dealing with, Manoah asks the 'angel' a question:

JDG 13:17-18 MKJV

> (17) And Manoah said to the Angel of Jehovah, What is Your name, so that when Your sayings come to pass we may do You honor?

> (18) And the Angel of Jehovah said to him, Why do you ask after My name in this way? Yea, it is Wonderful.

Judging from the hints we are given here in this text, we might easily surmise that Manoah was not simply visited by just any angel, but by the pre-incarnate Jesus himself! When asked for His name, His reply was 'Wonderful'. Shifting over to Isaiah chapter 9, we recall a verse that we hear at every Christmas play!

ISA 9:6 MKJV

> (6) For to us a Child is born, to us a Son is given; and the government shall be on His shoulder; and His name shall be called Wonderful, Counselor, The mighty God, The everlasting Father, The Prince of Peace.

Jesus, the Savior of the World, is called Wonderful! Wow! So maybe He was around at Creation... and after... and between... and all of the above! Perhaps this does not greatly shift our theology, but instead it may give us a deeper knowledge of who He is!

COMPILING ACCOUNTS

The scriptures were written by many different writers at many different times, and all of this was later bound into a leather-clad book as we now carry. If we are going to get the full story, we must search out the full story. A prime example is the story of the giving of the Ten Commandments to Moses.

In Exodus 31 and 32, we discover that Moses climbed the mountain and received the stone tablets written by God Himself. It is a highly detailed account of the story. However, we also find that in Deuteronomy chapter 9, Moses recounts the story and fills in some details we didn't get at first. For instance, one of my biggest questions at the end of the Exodus account is why did Aaron get off so easily?

EXO 32:35 MKJV

(35) And Jehovah plagued the people because they made the calf, which Aaron made.

In fact, it seems that the people were harshly punished while Aaron really scraped by with only a slapped hand. But when we pull up the extra details of the Deuteronomy story, we find this:

DEU 9:20 MKJV

(20) And Jehovah was very angry with Aaron to have destroyed him. And I prayed for Aaron also at the same time.

So it serves us well to remember that many Bible stories are repeated throughout scripture. Many of the Kings stories are repeated in Chronicles. The Babylonian captivity is spoken of by nearly all the prophets, major and minor, from different vantage points. We have already discussed the Gospels and how most contain the same content but with very different aspects. Let's touch on this briefly.

THE GOSPELS

Each of the Gospel writers wrote of the ministry of Jesus using different amounts of detail and different perspectives. Why, if this book is ultimately under the authorship of the Holy Spirit, would God want these perspectives? Subtle differences often create seemingly troublesome conundrums, especially to skeptics who are looking for reasons to discount the authenticity of scripture. Why would God give them fuel for this fire? I would again point out that God hides things for us, not from us. For those who are hungry, they shall again discover the signature of the Holy Spirit! For those who are looking for wood to fuel their skepticism, they too shall find! I will touch on this in my chapter about the Skeptic Plan.

Luke was a physician. His description of Jesus was one of Jesus the Man. His genealogy in Luke 3 was one that traced Jesus' physical bloodline all the way back to Adam. Yes, Jesus was fully human! On the other hand, Matthew concentrated on the kingly aspects of Jesus' ministry. His genealogy (Mat 1) traced the bloodline only as far as Abraham, for this was proof enough that Jesus had the 'right' to be King. Mark's perspective of Messiah was that of a servant. He listed no genealogy because nobody traces the genealogy of a slave – it's irrelevant. John's focus was on the deity of Jesus. He, too, excluded a genealogy because God has no beginning! Do you see the pattern? It's not possible to arrive at these conclusions unless we compile the accounts of Jesus' ministry. No, it's not an overly quick process.

These 'personas' of Jesus were signified in scripture as banner emblems – much like school mascots. His human persona was signified with a man's face. His servant persona was signified with an ox – the burden bearer in the Hebrew culture. The kingly persona of Messiah was signified as a lion – the standard of many kingdoms even today. The final persona of Jesus' deity was personified with the face of an eagle. When we go to the book of Revelation, we notice a description of four angelic creatures that surround the throne of God.

REV 4:6-7 MKJV

(6) And a sea of glass was in front of the throne, like crystal. And in the midst of the throne, and around the throne, were four living creatures, full of eyes in front and behind.

(7) And the first living creature was like a lion, and the second living creature like a calf, and the third living crea-

ture had the face of a man, and the fourth living creature like a flying eagle.

From a non-religious perspective, this is exquisite authorship. The design of the text is amazing in that there is nothing to out-right suggest the existence of these four 'themes' throughout the gospels, and yet when we dig we find that these are undeniably present. And then, for the author to capture these themes in four imaginary beasts who celebrate the book's hero night and day in the throne room of heaven… this is incredible imagination that would rival or surpass even the greatest fiction writers of our day. Again, this is from a secular perspective! But there's more!

When we go back into history a few hundred years from the gospel writers, a man named Ezekiel also wrote a strange passage about what he saw in a vision:

EZE 1:5-10 MKJV

(5) Also out of its midst came the likeness of four living creatures. And this was how they looked; they had the like-ness of a man.

(6) And four faces were to each, and four wings to each.

(7) And their feet were straight feet; and the sole of their feet was like the sole of a calf's foot. And they sparkled like the color of burnished copper.

(8) And the hands of a man extended from under their wings on their four sides; and the four of them had their faces and their wings,

(9) joining each one to the other by their wings. They did not turn in their going; each one went toward the front of their face.

(10) And the likeness of their faces: the face of a man, and the face of a lion, on the right side to the four of them; and the face of an ox on the left side to the four of them; and the face of an eagle to the four of them.

This could present a quandary for the secular analyst. The options are to declare a very great coincidence, or to prove that the authors conspired on story detail, which is tampering, or to prove that the stories were altered years later to satisfy an unknown agenda. This, too, would be tampering. If we go with the explanation that this story was later 'tweaked' to reveal hidden Messianic themes, then we must give credit to the 'tweaker' for having perhaps the most ingenious mind to ever grace our planet. But... there's more!

In Numbers 2, we see that God instructs Israel to encamp on the four sides of the tabernacle. Each of the four camps has a banner associated with the corresponding camp 'leaders': Judah, Reuben, Ephraim, and Dan. Ironically, the emblems for these four tribes are the Lion, Man, Ox, and Eagle, respectively. Apparently, even the details of the camp of Israel, God's chosen people, have Messianic implications. From the secular view, the planning and construction of such a collage of facts, if before seemed nearly impossible, now seem absurd and unbelievable. To the one who believes this book is inspired under divine authorship, we have identified another signature of the Holy Spirit!

When compiling accounts, attack studying the scriptures with a slow, methodical approach. You have to let things soak in! Take notes, either in the margins of your bible or in a notebook. I do a lot of my bible reading on the PC, so I keep Notepad up and available for notes, which I later save to CD. When even seemingly trivial facts are allowed to establish in our memory banks, then we notice when themes are repeated in scripture. I remind you – this is not a quick process! Do not get discouraged! Read with the understanding that one verse can provide a lifetime of revelation. Trying to absorb much is not always best. Bits and pieces are easier to digest, and when you consider that these precepts repeat, absorbing one is just like absorbing many!

WRONGLY DIVIDING THE WORD

2TI 2:15 MKJV

> (15) Study earnestly to present yourself approved to God, a workman that does not need to be ashamed, rightly dividing the Word of Truth.

Timothy grew up with a Jewish mother and grandmother, but his father was Greek. In the culture that Timothy lived, it was okay to be Jewish, and it was okay to be Greek, but to be a half-n-half was not a good place to be. You were considered a half-breed to both sides! On the other side of the coin, the apostle Paul was more like a Jewish rabbinic superhero. He was trained under the one of the greatest and most renowned sages of that time, Gamaliel. Paul took Timothy under his wing and fathered him in so many ways, which bespoke of divine intervention from the start. Timothy found a grace under Paul's guidance that he had never known. There's little doubt that Timothy must have appreciated Paul's understanding of the scriptures, because that was the same measuring stick that society had used against him since his birth. Paul understood rightly dividing the scriptures and he passed this to his understudy, Timothy. The word that Timothy used here for 'dividing' was 'orthotomeo', which means to cut straight, or to dissect correctly.

What does it mean to 'wrongly' divide the word? From looking at the verse above, a person who is 'hired' to do a job is considered a workman. The workman who is ashamed is one who wrongly divides the word. Why? He does so for his own gain. History shows us that much insanity, suffering, and abuse has been wrought in the name of Christianity in order to bring someone unjust gains. The Crusades are a prime example. The Inquisition is another. These 'endeavors' were undertaken for personal gain and were justified improperly by wrongly dividing the word, or taking God's instruction out of context. Such an example might be the following:

1 KI 17:10-16 MKJV

(10) And he arose and went to Zarephath, and came in to the entrance of the city, and, behold, the widow was gathering sticks. And he called to her and said, Please, bring me a little water in a vessel so that I may drink.

(11) And as she was going to bring it, he called to her and said, Please, bring me a piece of bread in your hand.

(12) And she said, As Jehovah your God lives, I do not have a cake, but only a handful of meal in a pitcher and a little oil in a jar. And behold, I am gathering two sticks, so that I may go in and dress it for me and my son, so that we may eat it and die.

(13) And Elijah said to her, Do not fear, go. Do as you have said. But first make me a little cake of it, and bring it to me. And then make for you and for your son.

(14) For so says Jehovah, the God of Israel, The pitcher of meal shall not be emptied, nor shall the jar of oil fail, until the day that Jehovah sends rain on the earth.

(15) And she went and did according to the saying of Elijah. And she and he and her house ate many days;

(16) the pitcher of meal was not consumed, and the jar of oil did not fail, according to the Word of Jehovah which He spoke by Elijah.

This is just one of the many incredible things that happened to the prophet Elijah. However, many preachers and evangelists have in similar ways taught that giving a 'back-breaking' offering to their ministry would cause God to miraculously sustain the ones giving the offering. The problem with this teaching is that we assume God wishes to use the same method of provision for the giver if the giver gives 'their last cake'. That's a poor and dangerous assumption. I purposely left off a very important passage:

1 KI 17:8-9 MKJV

(8) And the Word of Jehovah came to him, saying,

(9) Arise, go to Zarephath which belongs to Sidon, and live there. Behold, I have commanded a widow to keep you there.

Now we see how incorrectly dissecting this passage of scripture could play into the designs of a greedy person. The only reason Elijah asked for the widow's last meal was because he already knew the outcome of her situation! He never would have done it otherwise.

IGNORANCE

Much damage has been done because of ignorance. If I could only count the number of times in my life I have had to "rewire" my brain because I discovered what I had always been taught was not the whole truth. I appreciate my upbringing very much. It absolutely got me where I am today! But I accepted a lot of things at face value that perhaps I should not have. I would wager that most of us have done this. As an example, we read in the Old Testament about the case of Sodom and Gomorrah and of their destruction. Reading the account in Genesis 19, most of us have heard that the sin of Sodom was that of homosexuality, and for this the city was destroyed. Yes, homosexuality was prevalent in Sodom. It was a scary-bad problem they had! It was so bad that Lot did what many of us would think unthinkable – he offered up his own daughters to the angry, perverse mob in order to save complete strangers. It was a bad situation in Sodom!

But Sodom was not destroyed because of homosexuality. Ezekiel the prophet revealed this:

EZE 16:49-50 MKJV

(49) Behold, this was the iniquity of your sister Sodom; pride. Fullness of bread and abundance of idleness was in her and in her daughters. Nor did she strengthen the hand of the poor and needy.

(50) And they were haughty and did abominable things before Me, so I turned away as I saw fit.

Isn't that interesting! God said the sin of Sodom was one of PRIDE, and that the inhabitants of Sodom did not take care of the poor people! Why, then, have so many "religious" people used the destruction of Sodom and Gomorrah as an excuse to attack gay people? I dare say that if God were to categorize sin in this way, choosing homosexuality might possibly win more grace from Him than would ignoring the needy. Remember, God promised not to destroy Sodom if Abraham could find but ten righteous in the city. But beyond this, the angel could not destroy it until Lot was safely out of it. Could it be that so many have wrongly divided the Word of God on this matter? To reassure you, God did say in the Law that homosexuality was an abomination to Him. But then He took all of this anger and judgment out on His Son, Jesus, in order to redeem any who are caught in this trap of a lifestyle. God is good!

WILLFUL BLINDNESS

Do you see how the word is twisted to fit an ungodly agenda? This is the mark of wrongly dividing the word. A man who lords authority over his wife and treats her as his servant might attempt to justify himself with the passage:

EPH 5:22-24 MKJV

(22) Wives, submit yourselves to your own husbands, as to the Lord.

(23) For the husband is the head of the wife, even as Christ is the head of the church; and He is the Savior of the body.

(24) Therefore as the church is subject to Christ, so let the wives be to their own husbands in everything.

The problem is one of selective reading. The very next verse instructs the husband in how he should treat his wife:

EPH 5:25 MKJV

(25) Husbands, love your wives, even as Christ also loved the church and gave Himself for it,

The scriptures go on – but no more is really necessary. For a man to love his wife as Christ loved the church is to abandon totally one's own desires and preferences for the sake of his wife's well-being and comfort. This issue at hand, again, is one of abuse. That's a strong word, but Timothy also warned us about those who would twist the Word of God to fit a personal agenda:

2TI 4:3-4 MKJV

(3) For a time will be when they will not endure sound doctrine, but they will heap up teachers to themselves according to their own lusts, tickling the ear.

(4) And they will turn away their ears from the truth and will be turned to myths.

Peter wrote these incredible words:

2PE 3:15-17 MKJV

(15) And think of the long-suffering of our Lord as salvation (as our beloved brother Paul also has written to you according to the wisdom given to him

(16) as also in all his letters, speaking in them of these things; in which are some things hard to be understood, which the unlearned and unstable pervert, as also they do the rest of the Scriptures, to their own destruction).

(17) Therefore, beloved, knowing beforehand, beware lest being led away with the error of the lawless, you fall from your own steadfastness.

Wow! Even though the scriptures – by Peter's own admission – are difficult to understand, those who deliberately twist them are unstable, unlearned, and they destroy themselves!

Jesus warred against this type of mentality that took the Law of Moses (the written scriptures of Jesus' time) and used it to control others. To Him, this was an abomination! Jesus was the perfect, walking fulfillment of the Law. He never broke it. However, in personifying it, He placed it in its proper order: Love God, love your neighbor as yourself, and let everything else fall beneath this. There were those in Jesus' day that grasped the Law as a tool in which to rule others, pretending all the while to be walking in compliance to it. They wrongly divided it! Jesus continually showed them how far short of compliance they actually were, and they hated Him for it. As the Apostle Paul later explains to us, the Law was meant to be the mirror that we stare into in order to see how Christ-like we are.

Are we going to be perfect in our doctrines one-hundred percent of the time? No, probably not. As the eyes of our understanding open and our vision clears, we see that things we used to believe staunchly we can no longer be quite so sure about anymore. Our attitude towards this should always be 'repent and proceed'! But in this, we should also be very careful in what ideas we war to protect. Scripture says that arguing amongst each other – especially as Christian siblings – is not only non-productive but it's wrong. Pride is the heart of it, because someone is trying to be *right*. Titus said:

TIT 3:9 MKJV

(9) But avoid foolish questions and genealogies and contentions, and strivings about the Law, for they are unprofitable and vain.

So does truth in doctrine really matter? Of course it does! But if we burn bridges in our relationships we have no means to further impart truth to people. Rightly divide the Word, speak truth, and love people.

WHAT ABOUT CONTRADICTIONS?

After studying for just a short time, we find things that appear contradictory. If we do not sort these properly, we end up setting ourselves up to draw improper conclusions. This is an aspect of wrongly dividing the word. I will not spend a lot of time debunking a lot of common accusations that scripture is full of contradictions. If taken at face value, it truly does look like it is. However, some very good books have been written by some extremely smart individuals that explain supposed biblical contradictions. One must understand that scripture as a whole reveals Jesus. The questions that were asked in the Old Covenant were answered by Jesus. The Old Testament was very harsh. Entire people groups were wiped out. There was no escaping judgment for many of the sins described in Torah. Today, many take a look at these judgments and conclude that God is not a loving god or He never would have enacted such judgment. When Achan took some money from a conquered foe and buried it in his tent, his entire family was stoned, burned, and buried (Joshua 7). This is highly offensive to a culture that would simply consider this petty theft, fining the perpetrator and placing him on probation. When dealing with that kind of offense, the point is easily (and frequently) missed. Sin has consequences, and these always sum up to death. Not only was this why a savior was needed, but it's also why *the* Savior was so highly anticipated.

There is a tension all throughout scripture that appears contradictory. The difference between the two covenants – old and new – paint that picture very clearly. Jesus knew this was a difficult concept to grasp.

MAT 5:38-39 MKJV

(38) You have heard that it was said, "An eye for an eye, and a tooth for a tooth."

(39) But I say to you, Do not resist evil. But whoever shall strike you on your right cheek, turn the other to him also.

This can be a difficult bridge to cross even with other Christians. If God's desire was to judge mankind for what he truly deserved, He never would have sent Jesus. What do you say to the skeptic when he voices this "contradiction" without understanding that Jesus was the answer to his riddle? He has wrongly divided the word. Suspicious reading helps us out here. Where the Law demanded justice, grace demands mercy because Jesus became our justice, and thus fulfilled the requirement of the Law!

One of my brothers was at a gas station not very long ago. He was wearing a Florida hat which was a souvenir from a trip he'd taken long ago. He was met by a man who was obviously drunk. The drunk fellow was rather obnoxious and became insulting and borderline abusive about my brother's hat. This is where we discover why the scriptures say, "Be not drunk with wine." My brother is 6'-4 and looks quite athletic. Beyond that he is a multi-tour war veteran who has been trained to deal with adversaries – armed or not – drunk or not. My brother chose to walk away. He turned the other cheek, showing MUCH mercy to the drunkard. One might argue that a normal Christian would have no such options in a situation like that. After all, how many of us are trained in hand-to-hand combat?

MAT 26:51-53 MKJV

(51) And, behold, one of those who were with Jesus stretched out his hand and drew his sword, and he struck a servant of the high priest and cut off his ear.

(52) Then Jesus said to him, Put up your sword again into its place; for all who take the sword shall perish with a sword.

(53) Do you think that I cannot now pray to My Father, and He shall presently give Me more than twelve legions of angels?

Again we see a tension. We know from the other gospels that our mysterious swordsman here was none other than Peter. So here is a question. Why was Peter packing a sword?

LUK 22:34-36 MKJV

(34) And He said, I say to you, Peter, the cock shall not crow this day before you shall deny knowing Me three times.

(35) And He said to them, When I sent you without purse and wallet and sandals, did you lack anything? And they said, Nothing.

(36) And He said to them, But now, he who has a purse, let him take it, and likewise his wallet. And he who has no sword, let him sell his garment and buy one.

Peter was packing because Jesus told him to go buy a sword! The lesson that Peter learned was just because the Lord asks you to buy a sword, does not mean you are free to use it whenever you like. You must wait to use the sword until such time the Master tells you to use it. It's the lesson of the 'last cake' again. You do not tell someone to give a back-breaking offering unless the Lord has told you to do it! If you have assumed God's method because of past experiences, you've made a poor assumption.

END FROM THE BEGINNING

ISA 46:8-10 MKJV

> (8) Remember this, and be a man; return it on your heart, O sinners.

> (9) Remember former things from forever; for I am God, and no other is God, even none like Me,

> (10) declaring the end from the beginning, and from the past things which were not done, saying, My purpose shall stand, and I will do all My pleasure;

All those who seriously study the scriptures note the patterns that are found within. As I like to say, God is a God of patterns. In the case of prophecy, God tells us in Isaiah that He declares the end from the beginning and from the ancient times things that are not yet... There is a pattern. What exactly does He mean by this? The Hebrew says it like this: "magid mereshiyt acharit", or declaring out of the beginning, the end. It could be explained that the end comes out of the beginning as a fruit comes out of a seed – or as a great oak comes out of an acorn! Is that an intriguing thought? Somewhere in the beginning... the end exists. Hmmm!

If this is true, then the beginning is actually the *beginning of the end!* We must understand the beginning, or we will never understand the end.

Solomon wrote:

ECC 1:9-10 MKJV

(9) That which has been is that which shall be; and that which has been done is that which shall be done; and there is nothing new under the sun.

(10) Is there a thing of which it may be said, See, this is new? It has already been in days of old, which were before us.

In my view, this satisfies our golden rule requirement. But we need to find some examples of what is meant here! First, I would like to show you a passage that implies repetition:

JOE 2:23 MKJV

(23) Be glad then, sons of Zion, and rejoice in Jehovah your God. For He has given you the former rain according to righteousness, and He will cause the rain to come down for you, the former rain and the latter rain in the first month.

James also talks about this in his letter (James 5:7). The significance of this passage is that creation is designed with a pattern in mind. It rains in the spring, and then it rains in the fall. Don't think 'rain shower', think monsoon, or rainy season. The rains are for different purposes, agriculturally, but they serve to mark time for men who need to know when to plant, when to reap, and when to celebrate it all! We also realize from this design that it's normal when the rains come twice in a year, and NOT normal when the rains do not come or when it rains too much. Does this ever happen? Yes! Why? This is the purpose of establishing patterns. They prompt us to explore the questions.

HELD BY YOUR ORIGIN

When we speak of the end being determined from the beginning, I am prompted to start at the beginning in my search for clues as to what this means. I start with Adam. Adam came from the earth ('adamah' in the Hebrew). When sin entered the picture, Adam was told that he would die and return to the earth (Gen 3:19). Jesus was referred to as 'the second man, Adam'. He was not taken from the earth, but conceived through the Holy Spirit upon the virgin, Mary. The result of His origination is that after He died, the earth could not hold Him, but rather He was received back into heaven. We can only return to – or be held by - our place of origin. Jesus tried to explain this to Nicodemus:

JOH 3:13 MKJV

(13) And no one has ascended up to Heaven except He who came down from Heaven, the Son of Man who is in Heaven.

This sheds light upon the ingenuity of marriage, as woman was taken from man:

GEN 2:23-24 MKJV

(23) And Adam said, This is now bone of my bones and flesh of my flesh. She shall be called Woman because she was taken out of man.

(24) Therefore shall a man leave his father and his mother, and shall cleave to his wife and they shall be one flesh.

41

The woman can actually become one flesh with man because he is her place of origin. Those born of the Spirit of God (born again) then are able to establish a new spiritual origin, and even if the flesh dies, the earth cannot hold their body except on a temporary basis (1 Thessalonians 4:16). Jesus said this in so many words when asked by the Pharisees whether or not it was lawful to pay tribute to Caesar (Matthew 22:17). He knew they were setting a snare for Him and asked them to present a coin, which they did. His question to them was, "Whose is this image and superscription?" They replied, "Caesar's." To which He said… then it must belong to Caesar! We belong to the one who's image we bear.

Man was patterned (Gen 1:26) after the image of God. Because God is a ruler, the template of humanity is of ruler-ship by default:

Gen 1:28 MKJV

(28) And God blessed them. And God said to them, Be fruitful, and multiply and fill the earth, and subdue it. And have dominion over the fish of the sea and over the fowl of the heavens, and all animals that move upon the earth.

The significance of why man was created cannot be overstated. It was to have dominion and stewardship over the earth, and to populate it. When we study this design and wonder about the viability of the pattern, we must ask ourselves a question. If the end is determined from the beginning, and we know part of our purpose as the Body of Christ is to rule and reign as a Kingdom of Priests upon earth (Revelation 5:10), what steps do we take as believers to begin exercising this step in faith? Have we begun to reclaim dominion of the earth as we were originally commissioned, or are we waiting for something? Creation, apparently, is awaiting someone to take charge that is worthy!

Rom 8:19-21 MKJV

(19) For the earnest expectation of the creation waits for the manifestation of the sons of God.

(20) For the creation was not willingly subjected to vanity, but because of Him who subjected it on hope

(21) that the creation itself also shall be delivered from the bondage of corruption into the glorious liberty of the children of God.

THE GARDEN

Well, all this is fine and dandy! But is it a future thing or a present thing? According to the Genesis creation account, we were to watch after the Garden of Eden. We were gardeners! When Jesus resurrected from the dead, He was an example of what we are to be – a down-payment, if you will. That's why He was our First Fruits. First Fruits was a presentation, or tribute, of ripened crops to the God given in thanks for the sustenance. It was a thank you to God that *more was to come!* The followers of Jesus are known as His body and all expect to resurrect – just as He did. How was Jesus seen for the first time after His resurrection? Mary had gone to His tomb early in the morning. Finding it empty, she began to weep. When He spoke to her, she thought he was a gardener! Yes, we are to be like Him! We are to again step into the roles of caretakers of His creation. The fact is that when Jesus 'restores' all things, then we will again have full dominion over the earth. A mystery is how we will then be fruitful and multiply in our newly restored earth. The end result can be seen by looking at what we were in the beginning!

SPIRITUAL REPRODUCTION

Part of the command to Adam and Eve was to be fruitful and multiply. How does that look now? Goodness knows that the normal Christian family probably does not take that command as seriously as people do in other cultures. In fact, the Western culture has placed garnering wealth ahead of rearing large families. But there is certainly another aspect of this that I strongly suspect is the greater truth at work, and that is spiritual parenting. When the angel Gabriel announced to the priest Zacharias the coming of the Messiah, he said these words:

LUK 1:17 MKJV

(17) And he shall go before Him in the spirit and power of Elijah, to turn the hearts of the fathers to the children, and the disobedient to the wisdom of the just, to make ready a people prepared for the Lord.

Gabriel is talking about spiritual fathers and mothers who would rise up a generation of children that were zealous for the Lord. Being a spiritual parent is more important in so many ways than being a parent biologically. For one, your child-bearing years are much longer! One should never retire from this task. The ramifications of bearing (and rearing) spiritual offspring cannot be determined in this life, but we know from scripture that the entire Jewish nation calls Abraham 'father'.

There is an old saying: Blood is thicker than water. This means that the bonds of family and ancestry are stronger than the bonds between unrelated people. I would venture to take this a step further. The blood of Jesus binds us in such a way that our spiritual bonds are by far greater than those of biological ancestry. If you have never been able to have children biologically, there is good news for you! There is nothing preventing you from reproducing spiritually through your union with Christ! Oh! But we must also take into account that whatever we do here through spiritual parenting is but a shadow of what we must do in the future, for all things have not yet been restored!

PATTERNED AFTER THE HEAVENS

Even after God restores the earth to be as the garden was, we find that much of what is on earth is patterned after what is in Heaven.

HEB 9:23-24 MKJV

(23) Therefore it was necessary that the patterns of things in the heavens should be purified with these, but the heavenly things themselves were purified with better sacrifices than these.

(24) For Christ has not entered into the Holy of Holies made with hands, which are the figures of the true, but into Heaven itself, now to appear in the presence of God for us.

When God instituted the sacrifices to be carried out by the priesthood in the dessert, He did so with painstaking detail. There aren't very many people that I've met who love to go home and read the book of Leviticus. Why is that? God's attention to detail is tedious! God, through Moses, told the priests to purify all the items to be used in the Tabernacle because they were to be Holy! The writer of Hebrews tells us that just as this was so, even so were the originals in Heaven purified, but with the blood of Jesus instead of the blood of lambs and goats!

I believe that this idea of earthly things being patterned after heavenly things is so intriguing because it gives us a little bit of insight into a place where most of us (I won't say all) have never been. Even more questions are raised. Are earthly things the same size as heavenly things, or are they miniature? Were the dinosaurs patterned after heavenly creatures? These are entertaining things to ponder, at least.

ENOCH

The account of Enoch is short. It can be found in the book of Genesis, chapter 5. Enoch is a fascinating character to me, because he was fulfilling his passion of seeking after and following God, and then something strange happened. He vanished. God just took him! Talk about an 'and suddenly'! Enoch was the seventh generation down from his great (several times over) grandfather, Adam. Seven generations... do you hear a hollow tile?

GEN 5:24 MKJV

(24) And Enoch walked with God, and then he was not, for God took him.

Some scholars argue that the earliest known prophecy of the Second Coming in the Bible was through Enoch, as recorded in the book of Jude.

JUD 1:14-15 MKJV

(14) And Enoch, the seventh from Adam, also prophesied to these, saying, Behold, the Lord came with myriads of His saints,

(15) to do judgment against all, and to rebuke all the ungodly of them concerning all their ungodly works which they ungodly did, and concerning all the hard things ungodly sinners spoke against Him.

Strangely enough, Enoch, whose disappearance very much reminds us of the raptured Church, gave us the first prophecy of the second coming of Jesus! So what else is significant about Enoch? Perhaps the meaning of his name: teaching. Just for fun, let's bullet-point some things out!

- The age begins
- 7 generations pass and 'teaching' disappears
- The church disappears (holding to a rapture view)
- A 7-year tribulation ensues soon thereafter
- The age ends

Now certainly there is room to argue any of these points, but what I wish to show you is that the end has been determined from the beginning. It's almost as if we were looking at history through a mirror. Finding patterns such as these can be a very exhilarating way to study!

Hidden Levels of Understanding

As you read and re-read scriptures, you will discover that there is very often more than meets the eye to a passage. It just 'feels' different. Have you ever rolled across a tile floor in a desk chair and realized that in certain areas, the hum of the wheels change? You know there's a hollow area beneath – or at least a different material. Reading the word is no different. Sometimes a passage just sounds *deep*!

Let's take a verse out of Genesis, for instance.

GEN 21:33 MKJV

(33) And Abraham planted a tree in Beer-sheba, and called there on the name of Jehovah, the everlasting God.

It's not the most captivating passage in the world. To fill you in on the details, Abraham just made a covenant with Abimelech, the king of the Philistines in Gerar where Abraham and his family were living. This is where Beer-sheba is located. So Abraham plants a tree? So what? There is obviously a meaning in that – the

49

floor sounds hollow. I might simply assume this is something one does after an ancient covenant is made. Not so!

Step one, check out some different translations. In the modern King James, 'tree' is pretty generic. Some translations state 'a grove'. That's worse. Other translations use something very specific: a tamarisk tree. When we look at the Hebrew definition in Strong's Concordance, we see that all of these can be so, but the only one that might help is the most specific: the tamarisk tree. What is so special about a tamarisk tree?

One never plants a tamarisk tree for one's self. It is a very slow-growing desert tree that requires some domestic attention and protection. Unlike other wilder varieties of desert trees, the tamarisk can be killed by goats or camels, and sometimes it needs to be watered. If you plant a tamarisk tree, you do it with your children or grand children in mind. Now why would Abraham plant a tamarisk tree right in the middle of Philistine territory? Because by faith, Abraham was acknowledging that his descendants would own and occupy the land that later became known as the Promised Land! Is that powerful! Knowing that the tree was a tamarisk, Abraham was also conceding that the enemy would occupy and steward the land until the time came for Israel to take possession.

Now, stop and analyze what we've done. We can hear the hollow sound coming from beneath the floor. We know there's more to the verse than meets the eye because it simply doesn't make sense when we read it. How much digging did we actually do?

1. We found the most specific verse available
2. We verified it with the Hebrew definition
3. We got out the encyclopedia and looked up tamarisk tree
4. We meditated on the context of the story

From this, we found a gold nugget from which you could preach a lengthy sermon – or several.

Now we can see the different levels of understanding that the text holds. There is a surface level, called the **exegetical layer**. This layer is pretty much anything you can learn from the story at face value. It is what it is. Abraham cut a covenant and then planted a tree. Neat! Moving on... As you can see, there isn't a lot of in-depth thinking to this layer, and that's okay. That is how we understand most of the scriptures at first. Think of it as simply a familiarization layer. Then there is a layer that makes a little more personal sense. This is called the ***rema layer***. For instance, concerning the previous story, perhaps your grandfather had planted a tamarisk tree and you grew up playing in and around it! It would have a special meaning to you, personally, that someone else may not understand. Then we have the third layer which is more in-depth still – it's the hollow spot in the floor. It's called the ***prophetic layer*** because it holds a message of hidden prophetic significance that must be dug up. This is why we call hidden biblical truths *nuggets*! You have to dig for them! The nugget in our previous story was that a tamarisk tree is a slow grower, and that it was a testimony of Abraham's faith that his children would one day occupy the land in which he camped as a guest. This is the prophetic layer of understanding.

Let's take an example from the New Testament writings. How about the parable of the Good Samaritan!

LUK 10:29-37 MKJV

(29) But he, willing to justify himself, said to Jesus, And who is my neighbor?

(30) And answering, Jesus said, A certain man went down from Jerusalem to Jericho and fell among robbers, who stripped him of his clothing and wounded him, and departed, leaving him half dead.

(31) And by coincidence a certain priest came down that way and seeing him, he passed by on the opposite side.

(32) And in the same way a Levite, also being at the place, coming and seeing him, he passed on the opposite side.

(33) But a certain traveling Samaritan came upon him, and seeing him, he was filled with pity.

(34) And coming near, he bound up his wounds, pouring on oil and wine, and set him on his own animal and brought him to an inn, and took care of him.

(35) And going on the next day, he took out two denarii and gave them to the innkeeper, and said to him, Take care of him. And whatever more you spend, when I come again I will repay you.

(36) Then which of these three, do you think, was neighbor to him who fell among the robbers?

(37) And he said, The one doing the deed of mercy to him. And Jesus said to him, Go and do likewise.

This time, let's just look at this parable using the three layers of understanding we have described.

EXEGETICAL LAYER

A man falls upon hard times while traveling. He is victimized by robbers and left for dead. A priest and a Levite walked by, both ignoring the man who obviously needed help. Then a Samaritan man walks by, sees the hurting man and helps him, displaying much kindness and care. Obviously, the Samaritan was kind to his neighbor while the others were not! (Note: this is what I learned in Sunday school, but it is NOT the answer to the question Jesus asked!)

REMA LAYER

A man fell upon hard times and was victimized by robbers on the highway. A priest and a Levite walked by and did nothing for him.

They were not good neighbors. As I was on my way in to work this morning, I passed a man who was obviously broken down on the side of the highway. His hood was up and he looked like he needed help, but I was in too much of a hurry to stop. I wasn't a good neighbor, either. I know firsthand what it's like to not be a good neighbor! Maybe next time I will try to be more like the Samaritan man. This is the rema layer, the kind of personal application that gives me a greater understanding of the story.

PROPHETIC LAYER

A certain man fell among robbers. In the Hebrew, 'man' is 'adam'. It would seem that 'adam' fell amongst robbers who stripped him and left him wounded and *half dead*. If I compare this 'adam' to the Adam that I know, the one in Genesis, I see some similarities. Adam was deceived into disobeying God. The deception was perpetrated by a robber, Lucifer (John 10:10). The result was that Adam realized he was naked in the same way the robber stripped his victim (Gen 3:10-11). Adam also died spiritually, even though he still lived physically, because the wages of sin is death (Rom 6:23). In this way, Adam was left *half dead*. The first man who came down the pike was a priest, but he would not help the dying man. There was a priesthood before the Levites came along that Abraham tithed to (Gen 14:18) but this priesthood would not grant an immediate solution to Adam's problem. The fact is the priest *could not* help the dying man, even if he wanted to. There were strict rules that prevented priests from touching anything – or anyone – who was unclean. Although this sounds harsh, to touch the dead or dying was considered an unclean practice. The second man to walk down the road was a Levite. The Levites were God's chosen tribe, picked to bear the mantle of priest for all of Israel. Yet, in all of this, they also could not present a permanent solution to man's (*adam's*) sin problem. Who should come down the road next but a Samaritan! A Samaritan was a man hated by the Jewish people of Jesus' day because of his lineage. A Samaritan was considered a half-breed – half Jewish, half gentile... not even human in some Jewish circles. But the Samaritan was willing and able to help the dying man! Really? How so, when the priest and the Levite were powerless to do it? Applying what scripture says, we know that Jesus Himself was the only real answer to our sin problem. How do the Samaritan and Jesus relate? Jesus was also a type of half-breed, in that He had Jewish blood but divine DNA. He was half man, half God (for the sake of His story), even if He was all man, all God, according to scripture. He stopped to help the dying man on the highway. How does the song go? Life is a highway... The story says he poured oil and wine on the wounds. This begs the question: who does this? Who would pour oil (the Holy Spirit) and wine (the blood of Jesus) on a wound? Only Jesus! He brought the injured man to an inn and instructed the innkeeper to take care of him, paying him two denarius. What is the significance of two denarius? Scripture says that a daily wage is one denarius (Matt 20:2). Scripture also says that a day to the Lord is as one thousand years (2 Pet 3:8). The Samaritan paid for only enough care for the injured man to last him two days, or millennially-speaking two thousand years, and then said he would return and settle the difference. The prophetic layer shows us that Jesus died for our sin, efficiently doing all that is necessary for our healing, and then set us up in the inn for two thousand years approximately – when He will return to settle up. Yes, we are the injured man on the side of life's highway. Is there a bit of prophetic significance to this story? Is there more we can glean? For instance... what does it mean that He will come back and *settle up*? How might he settle up? Did He not leave enough provision for the expenses of the injured guest? Or did He perhaps expect the guest to contribute once he realized he was *healed*? Perhaps one should break down exactly what the denarius bought us. Perhaps we should see some more passages about how God 'repays' (Rom 12:19, 2Th 1:6, Heb 10:30). This is the prophetic layer. As you can see, it's as deep as the deep blue sea. It's the hollow spot under the tile that goes clear to China!

At this point, I hope what you are saying is WOW! I'd like to suggest to you that this type of revelation proves God's word is not simply a compilation of human writings, but is a signature of the Holy Spirit! Think for just a moment about the planning that would have to be meticulously performed to make these details work as they do. Think again, about who would have had to make these plans. Remember, the idea that Jesus was the answer to mans' sin problem was not – and still is not – popular. Who, then, would have gone to the trouble to hide proof that He was who He claimed He was? Certainly not His enemies!

PRO 25:2 MKJV

(2) The glory of God is to hide a thing; but the honor of kings is to search out a matter.

Congratulations! You have another nugget for your purse! The thing about nuggets… you are most likely to find them where other people have not yet looked!

Have you ever been shopping for antiques or collectables? Many love this sort of thing. I can understand the draw. It's much like a treasure hunt. The goal is to find something that only you recognize as a treasure, purchase it inexpensively, and restore it to glory! That is easier said than done. The concept was not lost on Jesus, however. He loved (loves) the world of men. He saw worth in us, perhaps because we were created in the image of His Father. His stories exemplify this love, even if He was speaking about other things.

MAT 13:45-46 MKJV

(45) Again, the kingdom of Heaven is like a merchant seeking beautiful pearls;

(46) who, when he had found one pearl of great price, went and sold all that he had, and bought it.

Jesus spoke of a merchant who sought to purchase pearls. On an exegetical layer, this story makes good business sense. We read it, think "hmmm, okay", and continue on. On a rema layer, we might compare this to our search for antiques. The merchant is no different than we are on our hunt for a diamond in the rough. But at the prophetic layer, the painting starts to get some color. You see, Jews did not identify with pearl merchants. Pearls were 'unclean' because they came from oysters, one of the animals forbidden from consumption by Torah. A 'righteous' Jewish merchant would steer clear of such so as not to even be associated with anything unclean. And yet, Jesus chose to use a pearl merchant as the focal point in His story. Why? Perhaps Jesus viewed Himself as a pearl merchant. Did He not give all He had in order to obtain us? But the example goes deeper than that. The pearl itself is created within the oyster from a single grain of sand – an irritant. The processes that act upon that irritation within that 'unclean' environment start to have a beautiful effect upon the sand. As it beautifies, it increases in size – a process known as accretion. We know from scriptures that Jesus had this irritating effect upon a corrupt world. Despite this, many were attracted and clung to Him, and His church increased in size. As His plans come to fruition, we see the end result will be a pearl – something beautiful taken from something unclean. God symbolizes this metamorphosis by creating the very gates of His New Jerusalem from enormous pearls. These layers exist in nearly every concept that Jesus taught.

The Jewish Angle

The Bible is a Jewish writing. Very, very little of it was written by a non-Jewish author. To that end, it is very difficult to understand parts of the book without an understanding of Jewish and rabbinic culture and methodology. Once we discover even small details about why people thought as they thought and spoke as they spoke, the scriptures explode into fresh revelation! Let's take a look at some examples of this.

The Remez

MAT 19:24 MKJV

> (24) And again I say to you, It is easier for a camel to go through the eye of a needle than for a rich man to enter into the kingdom of God.

If I was your Sunday school teacher and I wanted to imply something, I might say, "It's easier for Jim to go through the eye of a needle than for a rich man to enter into the kingdom of God." What did I just say? I just called Jim a camel – or at least equated him with one – because my entire audience knows Matthew 19:24 and that I substituted Jim's name with 'camel'. Not very nice, especially for a Sunday school teacher!

Rabbis used (and still use today) this method of teaching scripture. It is called *remez*, or hint. Like in the above example, the teacher will use a partial verse within conversation or speech knowing fully that the targeted audience will deduce the omitted portion of the verse, which is often the condemning or convicting portion. An example of this is found in Matthew 21:

MAT 21:15-16 MKJV

(15) And when the chief priests and scribes saw the wonderful things which He did, and the children crying in the temple, and saying, Hosanna to the Son of David, they were angry.

(16) And they said to Him, Do you hear what these say? And Jesus said to them, Yes, have you never read, "Out of the mouth of babes and sucklings You have perfected praise?"

This looks like a harmless transaction. It was anything but! Jesus was quoting Psalm 8:2:

PSA 8:2 MKJV

(2) Out of the mouths of babes and sucklings You have ordained strength, because of ones vexing You, to cause the enemy and the avenger to cease.

Remembering that especially the chief priests and scribes knew the scriptures by heart, quoting half a verse to them as Jesus did would immediately bring to mind the second half of the verse, *"because of ones vexing You, to cause the enemy and the avenger to cease."* These men would have been infuriated because Jesus was effectually calling them enemies of God. The potential of the remez is amazing, as is the ingenuity of the rabbinic way of teaching and interacting. Nobody was better at this than Jesus. In order to comply with our own golden rule, we should take a look at another!

John the Baptist was in prison. He was frightened, because chances were good that he was going to die by the hand of Herod. So he asks Jesus this very cryptic question:

MAT 11:3 MKJV

(3) And they said to Him, Are You he who should come, or do we look for another?

To the western mind, we tend to overlook the directness of the question and skip straight to the absurdity that such a question was asked in the first place. However, John, a rabbi, was doing something very rabbinic. He was prompting Jesus for an answer that only Jesus would give. What he actually asked was, "Are you the King that is coming?" This is the remez, only this is a very difficult one to track down. In order to understand John's question, we have to know where in the text Messiah was referenced to as the 'King that is coming'. The reference is found in Zechariah:

ZEC 9:9-11 MKJV

(9) Rejoice greatly, O daughter of Zion; shout, O daughter of Jerusalem; behold, your King comes to you. He is righteous and victorious, meek and riding on an ass, even on a colt, the son of an ass.

(10) And I will cut off the chariot from Ephraim, and the horse from Jerusalem. And the battle bow shall be cut off, and He shall speak peace to the nations; and His dominion shall be from sea to sea, and from the River to the ends of the earth.

(11) You also, by the blood of Your covenant I have freed Your prisoners out of the pit in which is no water.

Why was John asking this in this way? Because the *King that is Coming* would set those free who were 'prisoners in the pit', and John was definitely this. That – in itself – is brilliant! Here is his question in western English, "Jesus, are you going to leave me in prison?"

What did Jesus say? In order to show you my emphasis, let me leave this in black and white:

MAT 11:4-6 MKJV

(4) Jesus answered and said to them, Go and tell John again those things which you hear and see:

(5) the **blind receive their sight,** and **the lame walk; the lepers are cleansed,** and **the deaf hear; the dead are raised,** and **the poor have the gospel proclaimed to them.**

(6) And blessed is he, whoever shall not be offended in Me.

If you do not think these men knew the text, this passage should prove to you differently. Jesus is referring to six different quotes (all emphasized above) from the prophet Isaiah, all of which John would have known by heart.

Emphasized references 1 & 4 (The blind receive their sight.)

ISA 42:6-7 MKJV

(6) I Jehovah have called You in righteousness, and will hold Your hand, and will keep You, and give You for a covenant of the people, for a Light of the nations;

(7) **to open the blind eyes**, to bring out the prisoners from the prison, those who sit in darkness out of the prison house.

Emphasized references 2 & 3 (The lame walk; the lepers are cleansed.)

ISA 33:23-24 MKJV

(23) Your ropes are loosened, they do not hold the base of the mast; they could not spread the sail. Then the prey of a great spoil shall be divided; **the lame take the prey.**

(24) **And an inhabitant, the people who live in it shall not say, I am sick;** iniquity is taken away.

Emphasized reference 5 (The dead are raised.)

ISA 26:19-20 MKJV

(19) **Your dead ones shall live,** *together with* my dead body they shall arise. Awake and sing, you who dwell in the dust; for your dew *is as* the dew of lights, and the earth shall cast out the dead.

(20) Come, my people, enter into your rooms and shut your doors around you; hide for a little moment, until the fury has passed by.

Emphasized reference 6 (The Gospel is preached to the poor.)

ISA 61:1 MKJV

(1) The Spirit of the Lord Jehovah *is* on Me; because **Jehovah has anointed Me to preach the Gospel to the poor;** He has sent Me to bind up the broken-hearted, to proclaim liberty to the captives, **and the opening of the prison to those who are bound;**

All of these are references of the sick being made well and the ropes loosened, the lame walking and the ropes loosened, blind eyes opened and the prisoner set free, those made to hear and the prisoner set free, the dead live while the people are beckoned, and the Gospel is preached while the prison doors open. Yet Jesus tells John, **"the blind receive their sight, and the lame walk; the lepers are cleansed, and the deaf hear; the dead are raised, and the poor have the gospel proclaimed to them."** What is missing? The captive is set free (Isa 61:1). *John, my friend, it is all true, but you are going to die in prison.*

Then Jesus goes on to say, "John, blessed is he..." what? Blessed is he *that isn't offended* because of these things. What things in our text are so obviously offensive? It is so very hard to know... unless we realize the Jewish angle. It is easy to become frustrated at our inability to pick up these unobvious Jewish references. Remember, scripture was written so that a mere babe could grasp the truth. It's the truth that is crucial. Everything else... is gold to be dug up. These are the treasures, and if they were easy to come by, everyone would be rich!

Jesus would even imply deep truths by His actions, demonstrating a type of 'physical remez' to prove a point.

JOH 8:3-9 MKJV

(3)   And the scribes and Pharisees brought to Him a woman taken in adultery. And standing her in the midst,

(4)   they said to Him, Teacher, this woman was taken in adultery, in the very act.

(5)   Now Moses in the Law commanded us that such should be stoned. You, then, what do you say?

(6)   They said this, tempting Him so that they might have reason to accuse Him. But bending down, Jesus wrote on the ground with His finger, not appearing to hear.

(7)   But as they continued to ask Him, He lifted Himself up and said to them, He who is without sin among you, let him cast the first stone at her.

(8) And again bending down, He wrote on the ground.

(9) And hearing, and being convicted by conscience, they went out one by one, beginning at the oldest, until the last. And Jesus was left alone, and the woman standing in the midst.

As long as I can remember, I have heard people speculate on what Jesus was doing when He wrote on the ground. Most people believe that He was writing the sins of the accusers on the ground. Why else would they be so convicted as to walk away? This is a great question! Let me set this up, briefly.

Now on the last day of the feast of Tabernacles, Jesus makes this proclamation:

JOH 7:37-38 MKJV

(37) And in the last day of the great feast, Jesus stood and cried out, saying, If anyone thirsts, let him come to Me and drink.

(38) He who believes on Me, as the Scripture has said, "Out of his belly shall flow rivers of living water."

Skip down a bit…

JOH 7:45-49 MKJV

(45) Then the officers came to the chief priests and Pharisees. And they said to them, Why have you not brought him?

(46) The officers answered, Never did any man speak as does this Man.

(47) Then the Pharisees answered them, Also, have you not been deceived?

(48) Is it not true that not any of the rulers or of the Pharisees have believed into him?

(49) But this crowd, not knowing the Law, is cursed.

Okay, did Jesus just proclaim to be the fountain of living waters? Yes! Did the Pharisees just reject the Fountain of Living Waters? Yes! As before mentioned, these scribes and Pharisees had all of the writings of the prophets memorized. Jeremiah popped into their minds!

JER 17:13 MKJV

(13) O Jehovah, the Hope of Israel, all who forsake You shall be ashamed. Those who depart from Me shall be written in the earth, because they have forsaken Jehovah, the Fountain of living waters.

Do you see the physical remez? Jesus wrote their names in the earth because they had forsaken Him, the Fountain of Living Waters, and they knew it! No doubt there was another aspect of this, being that Jesus probably knew their names by communication with the Holy Spirit. That would be enough to disarm just about anyone.

QUESTIONS AND ANSWERS

Another Jewish angle that is very easy to see in scripture is the one of questions and answers. To ask a question is rabbinic. To answer that question with a question is even more rabbinic! It's like Spiritual Jeopardy! Hebrew children in that culture were taught the 'art' of asking questions at an early age. This is why Jesus was found in the Temple (at age 12) "sitting in the midst of the teachers, both hearing them, and asking them questions" (Luke 2:46). This would have been the age that Jesus was learning this teaching technique! As a rabbi, Jesus' skill with asking questions was unsurpassed:

MAR 11:27-33 MKJV

(27) And they came again to Jerusalem. And as He was walking in the temple, the chief priests and the scribes and the elders came to Him

(28) and said to Him, By what authority do you do these things? And who gave you this authority to do these things?

(29) And Jesus answered and said to them, I will also ask of you one thing, and answer Me, and I will tell you by what authority I do these things.

(30) The baptism of John, was it from Heaven, or from men? Answer Me.

(31) And they reasoned within themselves, saying, If we shall say, From Heaven, he will say, Why then did you not believe him?

(32) But if we shall say, From men, they feared the people, for all held John to be a prophet indeed.

(33) And they answered and said to Jesus, We cannot tell. And answering Jesus said to them, Neither do I tell you by what authority I do these things.

The chief priests and the elders had questions, to which Jesus replied with another question. In order to continue conversing with Jesus, these men would have had to answer Him with yet another question. However, knowing they were trapped and out-gunned, they answered with a statement, "We cannot tell." At this point, the conversation was over.

THE GREATEST COMMANDMENT

After reading through the Gospels for a very short time, it becomes apparent that many were trying to trap Jesus in order to imprison or kill Him. Most of the time, they began this process by asking questions, as we saw above. However, there were times when they would ask Him legitimate questions that plagued them on a daily basis. In fact, it was the great rabbis that were most-often asked these questions, because it was through the instruction of these rabbis with authority that people felt secure in the way they lived before God and before men. Every Jew held Torah (specifically, the first five books of the Bible) in the highest of reverence. Every rabbi with great authority had his own personal views of how a person should live out Torah in his or her own life. This personal view of the rabbi was known as his 'yoke'. Depending on the rabbi, the yoke would differ. While one rabbi believed that remembering the Sabbath Day and keeping it holy was more important than honoring your father and your mother, another rabbi would disagree. This seems like a trivial argument until your father or mother needs help with an emergency – which could be considered work – on the Sabbath.

MAT 22:35-40 MKJV

(35) Then one of them, a lawyer, asked, tempting Him and saying,

(36) Master, which is the great commandment in the Law?

(37) Jesus said to him, You shall love the Lord your God with all your heart, and with all your soul, and with all your mind.

(38) This is the first and great commandment.

(39) And the second is like it, You shall love your neighbor as yourself.

(40) On these two commandments hang all the Law and the Prophets.

Many times this question of yoke appears in the Gospel.

LUK 14:3-5 MKJV

(3) And answering, Jesus spoke to the lawyers and Pharisees, saying, Is it lawful to heal on the sabbath day?

(4) And they were silent. And taking him, He healed him and let him go.

(5) And He answered them, saying, Which of you shall have an ass or an ox fall into a pit and will not immediately pull him out on the sabbath day?

First you will notice, again, that Jesus answered their question with a question. Secondly, we see that this struggle was one of a legalistic nature. Jesus did not teach a whirlwind of rules and regulations, which seemed to perplex the teachers of the Law. Instead, He made the claim, "My yoke is easy, and my burden is light." These conversations are somewhat difficult to process unless we do so from a Jewish angle.

A NEW COVENANT'S VALIDITY

Jesus was, by His own claim, King of the Jews. From a sheer faith standpoint, this is not difficult to swallow. After all, He was born of a virgin; He died, and was resurrected on the third day. If faith will allow us to believe this, then the claim of King isn't a problem for most Christian audiences! But for the Jew, it's a serious claim. What on earth would give anyone the right to make such a claim? It would need to be more than a symbolic declaration! It would have to be absolutely legal! Hence, we are posed a problem. What makes the Kingship of Jesus legal?

In most cultures and certainly in the Jewish culture, to be King was a family affair. Aside from God anointing the very first King of Israel, Saul, or from a sort of impeachment by God as also happened to Saul, being king was a matter of bloodline. If your father was king, his firstborn would be the next king.

The Messiah was prophesied to be a descendant of David (Isa 11:10, 2 Sam 7:12-16). The teachers of the Law knew these prophecies well!

JOH 7:42-43 MKJV

(42)   Has the Scripture not said that Christ comes from the seed of David and out of the town of Bethlehem, where David was?

(43) So a division occurred in the crowd because of Him.

As you can see from these passages, the topic was a matter of contention in the synagogues. Why would that be if not for the very claims made by Jesus? If royal blood was passed through the bloodline of the father, then we are immediately faced with a quandary. Jesus was not really the son of Joseph, so his lineage could not be confirmed in the traditional manner. If Jesus was to be a descendant of David in order to be a legal king, then we have to figure out what to do with the fact that His real Father was the Holy Spirit (Matt 1:18)!

The answer lay with His mother, Mary. There was a little story in the book of Numbers about a man named Zelophehad. He died without having any sons in which to pass on his inheritance. But he did have two daughters who went to Moses and asked why the inheritance should not fall to them. Moses took the matter to God, who agreed with the claim made by Zelophehad's daughters (Numbers 27:1-11). Here we find a hollow tile.

NUM 27:8 MKJV

(8) And you shall speak to the sons of Israel, saying, When a man dies, and has no son, then you shall cause his inheritance to pass to his daughter.

When we couple this verse with verse 4, it raises a question.

NUM 27:4 MKJV

(4) Why should the name of our father be taken away from among his family, because he has no son? Therefore give us a possession among the brothers of our father.

The daughters are asking about the 'name' of their father, and the Lord addresses the issue by granting them an inheritance of land. Yes, a land inheritance and the family name are equated here. God is saying that He is continuing the BLOODLINE through the daughters! But how... what...?

We learn in Numbers chapter 36 that there were some strings attached.

NUM 36:6-7 MKJV

(6) This is the thing which Jehovah commands concerning the daughters of Zelophehad, saying, Let them marry to whom they think best. Only they shall marry into the family of the tribe of their father.

(7) So the inheritance of the sons of Israel shall not be moved from tribe to tribe. For every one of the sons of Israel shall keep himself to the inheritance of the tribe of his fathers.

It was therefore of utmost importance to know from whom Mary descended, and also to know if she followed the rules when it came to marrying the proper person, Joseph! Now perhaps it makes sense as to why we have two separate genealogies in the

Gospels, one in Matthew 1 and the next in Luke 3. When we read the Matthew genealogy, we see that it begins with Abraham and goes all the way down through Joseph, where Joseph's father is mentioned as a man named Jacob. The problem with this lineage is that it is cursed because of a man named Jehoiachin, also known as Jeconiah, or Coniah (Matthew 1:11,12).

JER 22:30 MKJV

(30) So says Jehovah, Write this man (Coniah) down as childless, a man who will not be blessed in his days. For no man of his seed shall be blessed, sitting on the throne of David and ruling any more in Judah.

However, it does provide us proof that Joseph was from the tribe of Judah – one of our requisites for Jesus being King and Messiah! The Luke 3 genealogy gives us another lineage all the way from Adam to "Joseph, son of Heli", which seems to be a contradiction. However, because Mary has followed the rules established by God according to Zelophehad's daughters and has married within the tribe of Judah, her husband Joseph is the son 'in law' of Heli, Mary's father! The Luke 3 genealogy is that of Mary. It is un-cursed because it does not go through Jehoiachin and therefore fulfills the prophecy of Genesis 3 that Messiah should come through the seed of a woman!

GEN 3:15 MKJV

(15) And I will put enmity between you and the woman, and between your seed and her Seed; He will bruise your head, and you shall bruise His heel.

Was Jesus, then, legally able to make the claim of King of the Jews! He absolutely was! He was legally a descendant of Judah, from where the scepter should not depart (Genesis 49:10)!

GEZERAH SHEVA

'Gezerah Sheva' is another rabbinic teaching technique that links biblical texts that share exact phrases together to form a greater understanding of a specific topic. One of the most common examples is the linking of Deuteronomy 6:5 with Leviticus 19:18. Here they are:

DEU 6:5 MKJV

(5) And you shall love Jehovah your God with all your heart and with all your soul and with all your might.

LEV 19:18 MKJV

(18) You shall not avenge, nor bear any grudge against the sons of your people; but you shall love your neighbor as yourself. I am Jehovah.

The linking phrase is "you shall love". Jesus took these two and combined them into one teaching:

MAT 22:36-40 MKJV

(36) Master, which is the great commandment in the Law?

(37) Jesus said to him, You shall love the Lord your God with all your heart, and with all your soul, and with all your mind.

(38) This is the first and great commandment.

(39) And the second is like it, You shall love your neighbor as yourself.

(40) On these two commandments hang all the Law and the Prophets.

This line of thought makes good sense. If God is Love, then it would be illegal to claim His 'agape' (unconditional) love of Him and yet not love our neighbor. John said it this way:

1JN 4:20 MKJV

(20) If anyone says, I love God, and hates his brother, he is a liar. For if he does not love his brother whom he has seen, how can he love God whom he has not seen?

For this reason, many have said that the first requirement to loving God is to love your neighbor. It's the first hurdle, in a manner of speaking. As a point of interest, Jesus told John to write a letter to the church at Ephesus in which He said, "You left your first love" (Rev 2:4). From this it is rationalized that perhaps brotherly love within this congregation had waned. Loving your brother must come first if you are to love God, right?

Another example of Gezerah Sheva from a strictly Old Testament perspective can be found in the book of Numbers. Here we read about the prophet Balaam who is employed by the Moabite king Balak to curse Israel. I will discuss this more at length, later, but right on the onset of the story, Balak says something very interesting.

NUM 22:6 MKJV

(6) Therefore, I pray you, come now and curse this people for me. For they are too mighty for me. Perhaps I shall prevail so that we may strike them, and so that I may drive them out of the land. For I know that he whom you bless is blessed, and he whom you curse is cursed.

In the book of Genesis, God says this:

GEN 12:3 MKJV

(3) And I will bless those that bless you and curse the one who curses you. And in you shall all families of the earth be blessed.

Gezerah Sheva tells us that we should be comparing the wicked prophet Balaam to the righteous Abraham. Hmmm... WHY for goodness sake? What could they possibly have in common beyond the seemingly coincidental statement that they have the ability to bless and curse? Let's take a closer look. Both men took a trip – a journey – of sorts.

❖ Both men rose early and saddled their donkeys (Gen 22:3, Num 22:21)
❖ Their desires
  ➢ Abraham's desire was to obey God, even if it meant killing his son, Isaac. (Gen 22:10)
  ➢ Balaam's desire was to earn a paycheck, even if it meant slaying his donkey (Num 22:29)
❖ Both men's' hands were stayed by an angel (Gen 22:11, Num 22:31)
  ➢ Abraham was praised (Gen 22:16)
  ➢ Balaam was rebuked (Num 22:32)

We realize that by drawing such comparisons, faith, which seems to be such a blind attribute, actually gives sight to those who live by it. Genesis 22:13 says that "Abraham lifted up his eyes, and looked." Abraham could 'see' because of his faith. Contrary to this was Balaam, who being a 'prophet' was supposed to be able to see. His interest in self, however, did not even serve himself. He could not see that even the forces of heaven had come against him. Rather, it was his donkey that had the ability to see.

Employing Gezerah Sheva to hunt down comparisons like this is certainly not rocket science! Because this method is primarily eastern and rabbinic in nature, most of the results you will get from it will be new revelation to the western mindset! I challenge you to pay attention to phrases in the scriptures that are repeated and follow the trails back to where they originate! You will no doubt discover nuggets of great value!

NOTICE THE
NUMBERS

While reading along in scripture, notice that it is chock-full of numeric descriptions. For the most part, numbers seem to be important to the author for the sake of adding a little 'color' to the story. Especially in the Old Testament writings where unfamiliar units of measure are mentioned, we see that numbers might have meant something to a Jewish man who lived three thousand years ago, but have somehow lost their impact in our culture. Some numbers seem to be used in the most casual of senses. I would like to suggest, however, that in nearly every case the numbers that are used in scripture are very significant in spite of our inability to identify with the context in which they were used. Simply put – pay attention to the numbers!

Why is it that so many books have been written on Biblical numerology? The topic is big! It's far bigger than can be covered in a chapter here. But since this book is serving as a crash-course on studying scripture, we should take a look at how and why numbers are used. Let's start from the beginning. The very beginning!

In Genesis chapter 1 and 2, we see that the creation story is summarized – completely. It begins on day 1, and ends on day 7 when God rests from what He has done. Right off the bat, we can add a few drops of suspicion to our soup and hypothetically conclude that God may do many things in 7's. In fact, this is known as the number of completion because God 'completed' His creation work in seven days, the seventh day being the 'Sabbath', or day of rest. Others call this the number of perfection because his work was 'very good' (Gen 1:31). This causes us to ask our stand-by question: so what?

Allow me to get a little deeper for a moment. In the book of Exodus, God tells Moses to create a golden model of the burning bush. It's referred to as a lampstand in scripture, but today is known as a menorah. The menorah that Moses was instructed to make was like a large, golden candlestick with three branches coming out of two sides of it. So in all, it had seven 'lamps' on it.

EXO 25:32 MKJV

(32) And six branches shall come out of the sides of it– three branches of the lampstand out of

the one side, and three branches of the lampstand out of the other side.

The lampstand is a physical representation of God's design of creation and redemption! How so? First, it is important to know that the center 'candlestick' of the lampstand (the fourth candle) is known as the servant lamp, or 'shamesh'. It is the lamp from which all the other lights draw their oil. It's the source! Jesus is known as our 'suffering servant' (Isaiah 53:11). He, too, is the 'source' of 'oil' for us, as He made it possible for us to have a relationship with the Holy Spirit, commonly associated with oil. Jesus said, "I am the LIGHT of the world!" If we then associate the 4th lamp on the menorah with Jesus, we have quite a picture forming!

Going back to Genesis chapter 1, what happened on the fourth day? God made the 'sun' (Genesis 1:16)! The Hebrew word for 'sun' is 'shemesh', or 'brilliant light'. Considering that Hebrew is a language that does not have written vowels, the word 'shamesh' and the word 'shemesh' are identical. On day four, God created the 'sun'. Associate this with intense LIGHT, or FIRE! John saw Jesus, glorified, in the Revelation chapter one:

REV 1:13-14 MKJV

(13) And having turned, I saw seven golden lampstands. And in the midst of the seven lampstands I saw One like the Son of man, clothed with a garment down to the feet, and tied around the breast with a golden band.

(14) His head and hair were white like wool, as white as snow. And His eyes were like a flame of fire.

If there is no light, there is no life! Even in the parts of the earth where light is scarce, life gets to be scarce as well. Jesus, the light of the world (shemesh), is the source of life – the servant (shamesh) of the world as well. Both of these are signified by the fourth branch of seven. In Revelation 21:23, the New Jerusalem has no need of the sun (shemesh), because the Lamb of God (shamesh) is the light!

As we continue with this picture, understand that the Bible gives us a picture of history from the birth of Jesus all the way back to the creation of Adam. This expanse of time from Adam to Jesus is approximately 4,000 years. If the creation week was seven days long and God created the sun on day four, then which millennium did Jesus (the Son) arrive? The fourth, naturally, approximately 2,000 years ago! Again, if the timeline of world history is set above a menorah lampstand, each lamp would be 1,000 years. Jesus' arrival would be dead center over the middle lamp, or servant lamp. Oh, but it just goes on and on! If we look at LIGHT in general, any 3rd grade art student will tell you that the spectrum of known light is comprised of the seven colors in a rainbow. Do you remember ROYGBIV? Red, orange, yellow, green, blue, indigo, and violet are the colors. Which is color number four? Green!

When John described the One who sat on the throne in the book of the Revelation, he described it this way:

REV 4:3 MKJV

(3) And He who sat there looked like a jasper stone and a sardius. And a rainbow was around the throne, looking like an emerald.

The rainbow was 'around' the throne, while He who sat upon it was as an 'emerald'. Green! To give you one more example as to the depth of seven in scripture, let's take a quick look at the High Holy Days, or feast days, given to Moses. They were these, in order: Passover, Unleavened Bread, First Fruits, Pentecost, Trumpets, Day of Atonement, and Tabernacles. Of the seven, which is the fourth? Pentecost! And what happened on the day of Pentecost? Flames (shemesh) of fire appeared!

ACT 2:3 MKJV

(3) And tongues as of fire appeared to them, being distributed; and it sat upon each of them.

This should serve to make us suspicious of any mention of the number seven in scripture. We know that in Revelation, John dictated letters to the seven churches of Asia Minor. The seven churches written to in chapters 2 and 3 are: Ephesus, Smyrna, Pergamos, Thyatira, Sardis, Philadelphia, and Laodicea. The immediate question is... what is church number four and does it have 'anything' to do with "shemesh", or fire?

REV 2:18 MKJV

(18) And to the angel of the church in Thyatira write: The Son of God, He who has His eyes like a flame of fire and His feet like burnished metal, says these things:

Okay, I think that is almost enough of seven. But in one last example we find that four is not always obviously associated with seven. For instance, in the book of Daniel, most of us know the story of the three Hebrew children, oddly enough known by the

Babylonian names Shadrach, Meshach, and Abednego. When Nebuchadnezzar grew angry with them for refusing to bow before his golden image, he had them thrown into the fiery furnace. Again, we see fire. Recall, then, that a fourth person showed up. Who was it?

DAN 3:25 KJV

(25) He answered and said, Lo, I see four men loose, walking in the midst of the fire, and they have no hurt; and the form of the fourth is like the Son of God.

For those of you who already knew this story, have you ever wondered how a man like Nebuchadnezzar, a pagan king, knew what Jesus might look like? It is definitely another angle to search!

It is so fun to search scriptures for these patterns! What about the use of other numbers? Three is known as the number of perfection and completion also, as God is described as 'triune': God the Father, God the Son, and God the Holy Spirit. Six is the number of man, or one short of perfection. When reading about Goliath (1 Sam 17:4), you will notice that odd things are described about him, such as the weight of the tip of his spear. His height is described as well. Three descriptions are given with various multiples of six, which, to the Jewish mind simply says that Goliath was the devil's man. Again, in the Revelation we know that the mark of the beast is a 'human' number: 666. Six – three times – or perfectly imperfect... This is a good example of biblical mathematics.

Forty is the number of trial, or cleaning. It rained upon the earth 40 days and 40 nights when the world flooded. Israel wandered the desert for 40 years because of their unbelief. Jesus fasted in the desert 40 days and was tested by the devil. God gave 10 commands to Moses. Jacob had 12 sons, even as Jesus called 12 disciples. Paul described the 5-fold ministry. These numbers are all significant and should be noticed as you read. As you can see, there is often a tie-in to Old Testament and New Testament references to these numbers.

THE IMPERFECTION OF SIX, THE PERFECTION OF SEVEN

In the book of Numbers (no pun intended), we are introduced to the idea of cities of refuge. The purpose of these cities was to provide safe-haven for anyone accused of manslaughter, or accidental killing. If a person killed another person by accident, they were allowed to flee into one of SIX cities, designated by Moses. There, the person was determined to be guilty (of murder) or innocent (guilty of manslaughter) by the priests. If innocent, they were allowed to stay in that city until the death of the High Priest. If guilty, they were turned over to the 'avenger of blood' which was typically a relative of the slain individual who was out for vengeance. Likewise, if the innocent individual left the city of refuge before the death of the High Priest, his blood was on his own hands because he stepped out from under the protection of the law. Joshua chapter 20 lists these six cities.

There is a seventh city of refuge that scripture identifies in a round-about way.

HEB 6:17-20 MKJV

(17) In this way desiring to declare more fully to the heirs of promise the immutability of His counsel, God interposed by an oath,

(18) so that by two immutable things, in which it was impossible for God to lie, we might have a strong consolation, who have fled for refuge to lay hold upon the hope set before us,

(19) which hope we have as an anchor of the soul, both sure and steadfast, and which enters into that within the veil,

(20) where the Forerunner has entered for us, even Jesus, having become a high priest forever after the order of Melchizedek.

As you can see, the writer of Hebrews is speaking of refuge and also identifies our High Priest, Jesus. The Body of Christ, the Church, is often referred to as a city (Revelation 21:9-10). The differences are these: Those who ran to the six cities had to be innocent, and even so had to stay within the confines of their city until the death of a mortal High Priest. Those who run to the refuge of Jesus are GUILTY, and yet our High Priest has already died and will forever make intercession for us. Do you see how the imperfection of the six cities fails to compare to the perfection of the seventh?

THE BIBLE CODE

When discussing Biblical numerology, inevitably the question arises: what about the Bible code? The Bible code is the idea that there is a mathematical design to scriptures that conceals truths that can be obtained in no other way than to crack the code. First of all, the Bible is a very mathematical book and has a ton of symmetry in it. It's undeniable. Many very smart individuals have written books on this subject. Dr. Chuck Missler is one author and Bible teacher who has done much research on some 'codes' found within scripture and he does a fantastic job of explaining these. I would like to make a simple point about this, however. The symmetry found in scripture proves this is not a book simply authored by a bunch of men. The codes prove that the author is God, as it is mathematically impossible to produce (or reproduce) this type of writing through human means, especially over the course of hundreds of years and with no cooperation from the participating scribes.

There is no concealed code which contradicts what the book teaches! Any attempt to identify a code that states Jesus was married and had thirty children is in vain and is contrived by movie producers. The study of 'codes', or mathematical symmetry within scripture, is truly fascinating but is a topic that expands well-beyond what I am trying to address here.

Rabbit Trails

Some folks get disturbed whenever they begin to study a topic in the bible and end up on what I call a rabbit trail. Rabbit trails are what we follow whenever we become distracted from our original purpose of study because a different topic jumps out at us. This happens to me all the time, but I have totally made peace with it. I came to the understanding that the Holy Spirit leads me when I am in the Word, and even if I had a pre-conceived plan, I had better be willing to abandon it in order to let Him show me something new. So... down the rabbit trail I go!

This even happened to me multiple times while penning this book. It has become a way of life for me in my study of scriptures. In a way, a willingness to follow a rabbit trail before beginning my study makes studying the Word far more exciting and enjoyable. There is a relaxed quality to this approach, and I think the Holy Spirit often is able to work with me to a greater degree when I am not stressed about staying on-course, so to speak. What does it look like, exactly, to follow a rabbit trail?

To begin with, I really love to use Bible software in order to study. The reason for this is that the search capabilities are so much faster than sitting down with a huge concordance. I can bring up every instance of a word or phrase (or even a Strong's number) in a matter of seconds. This really lends itself to rabbit-trailing!

Another tool I use a lot is a good internet search like Google or Bing. I have a lot of words floating around in my head and most of them are in mixed translations, so when it comes time for me to do a search, I run into problems with matching the word in my head with the word in the translation I am searching. The answer – for me - is Google! Google not only returns exact matches, but it returns possible matches, including other people who wrote articles with the same (sometimes mistaken) wording of verses. This is so very handy!

One rabbit trail I found myself on recently had to do with names and how God addresses those who follow Him.

LUK 22:31 MKJV

(31) And the Lord said, Simon, Simon, behold, Satan has desired you, that he may sift you as wheat.

The reason that this became a rabbit trail is two-fold. One, Jesus had already decided not to call Simon by that name any longer. He had named him Peter. But now He calls him Simon again! Why? As well, there is another interesting question that arises. What is the significance of Jesus saying Simon twice? Simon, Simon...

Talk about a rabbit trail! This one branches off all over the place! Simon means 'a reed' – something that is blown about by the wind. When Jesus named him Peter, or 'Petros', he was naming him Rock, or something not easily blown about. Why the shift? How was Peter acting?

LUK 22:33-34 MKJV

(33) And he said to Him, Lord, I am ready to go with You, both into prison and into death.

(34) And He said, I say to you, Peter, the cock shall not crow this day before you shall deny knowing Me three times.

We see that Peter was being blown around a bit here. Jesus was telling him that soon He would be delivered up to the authorities, and Peter was very conflicted. His desire was to follow Jesus to the death, but we all know what happened instead. Peter did indeed deny Jesus three times. Now, how about the significance of Jesus speaking his name twice? Who else did this happen to?

GEN 22:10-11 MKJV

(10) And Abraham stretched out his hand and took the knife to slay his son.

(11) And the Angel of Jehovah called to him from the heavens and said, Abraham! Abraham! And he said, Here am I.

ACT 9:3-4 MKJV

(3) But in going, it happened as he drew near to Damascus, even suddenly a light from the heaven shone around him.

(4) And he fell to the earth and heard a voice saying to him, Saul, Saul, why do you persecute Me?

1SA 3:10 MKJV

(10) And Jehovah came and stood, and called as at other times, Samuel, Samuel! Then Samuel answered, Speak, for Your servant hears.

GEN 46:2-3 MKJV

(2) And God spoke to Israel in the visions of the night, and said, Jacob, Jacob! And he said, Here I am.

(3) And He said, I am God, the God of your fathers. Do not fear to go down into Egypt, for I will make of you a great nation.

EXO 3:4 MKJV

(4) And Jehovah saw that he had turned aside to see. God called to him out of the midst of the thorn bush, and said, Moses! Moses! And he said, Here I am.

The first thing I notice about several of these accounts is that some of these individuals had their name changed by God. Abraham had been Abram. Jacob became Israel. Simon became Peter. Is this a coincidence? It is possible, but inconclusive because of Samuel and Moses. What we do learn, however, is that whenever God calls your name twice, He is about to bring something to pass.

- God revealed to Abraham His plan to make a nation from his seed and bless it forever because of his obedience to offer his son, Isaac.
- God made Saul (later Paul) a purveyor of the Kingdom to the gentiles.
- God passed judgment upon the sons of Eli, elevating Samuel to a great prophet and judge over Israel.
- God promised Jacob that he and his sons would go to Egypt to live for a long season, but would be greatly blessed.
- God declared to Moses that he would deliver Israel from the bondage of Egypt.
- God declared that Peter would be tried by the devil, but that He would emerge from the trial because He had prayed for Peter.

In each case, God was about to declare something to be that was not – yet. Oh dear, that reminds me of another verse:

ROM 4:17 MKJV

(17b) –before God, whom he believed, who makes the dead live, and calls the things which do not exist as though they do exist.

Do you see that we are on a rabbit trail? My next inclination is to go to Genesis chapter one and begin reading about how God called things into existence that were not yet in existence. Go ahead! Wear yourself out doing this and you will sleep well tonight! You may even discover that the Holy Spirit has taught you many things in the process!

I was recently studying about Balaam and his donkey encounter. I've written about that in detail in other chapters of this book. For some reason, though, I decided to do a search on donkey – I suppose because I was so intrigued by how God used the donkey in that story. What I found spoke to me in a profound way, so let me share. There are ten verses in Numbers 22 that talk about the donkey. I will show you these from the Good News Translation:

1. (Num 22:21 GNT) So the next morning Balaam saddled his donkey and went with the Moabite leaders.

2. (Num 22:22 GNT) God was angry that Balaam was going, and as Balaam was riding along on his donkey, accompanied by his two servants, the angel of the Lord stood in the road to bar his way.

3. (Num 22:23 GNT) When the donkey saw the angel standing there holding a sword, it left the road and turned into the fields. Balaam beat the donkey and brought it back onto the road.

4. (Num 22:25 GNT) When the donkey saw the angel, it moved over against the wall and crushed Balaam's foot against it. Again Balaam beat the donkey.

5. (Num 22:27 GNT) This time, when the donkey saw the angel, it lay down. Balaam lost his temper and began to beat the donkey with his stick.

6. (Num 22:28 GNT) Then the Lord gave the donkey the power of speech, and it said to Balaam, "What have I done to you? Why have you beaten me these three times?"

7. (Num 22:29 GNT) Balaam answered, "Because you have made a fool of me! If I had a sword, I would kill you."

8. (Num 22:30 GNT) The donkey replied, "Am I not the same donkey on which you have ridden all your life? Have I ever treated you like this before?" "No," he answered.

9. (Num 22:32 GNT) The angel demanded, "Why have you beaten your donkey three times like this? I have come to bar your way, because you should not be making this journey.

10. (Num 22:33 GNT) But your donkey saw me and turned aside three times. If it hadn't, I would have killed you and spared the donkey."

I also found these other verses in my search. I will switch back to the Modern King James for clarity:

JDG 15:15-19 MKJV

(15) And he found a new jawbone of an ass, and put forth his hand and took it, and killed a thousand men with it.

(16) And Samson said, With the jawbone of an ass, heaps upon heaps, with the jawbone of an ass I have killed a thousand men.

(17) And it happened when he had made an end of speaking, he threw away the jawbone out of his hand, and called that place Hill of the Jawbone.

(18) And he was very thirsty and called upon Jehovah and said, You have given this great deliverance into the hand of Your servant. And now shall I die with thirst, and fall into the hand of the uncircumcised?

(19) But God cut open a hollow place and water came out there. And he drank, and his spirit came again, and he revived. Therefore, its name is called Fountain of the Praying One, which is in Lehi to this day.

In the case of Balaam's donkey, the donkey would not let Balaam proceed as he would have liked. Verse 9 in the English Standard Version has the angel stating that Balaam's way was 'perverse'. In the second story, Samson used the jawbone (mouth) of a donkey once again in the destruction of the perverse. Do you see a pattern? Oh, but it gets a little meatier! Samson, I know from previous study, is a picture of Jesus. What? Yes! His birth was announced by an 'angel' to his mother, just as Jesus' birth was announced to Mary. His mother was barren; therefore the birth was to be miraculous. He was to be a Nazarite, even as Jesus was from Nazareth. But you say Samson was a total cut-up who ended up in disaster! True! Jesus also 'became sin' and was killed – but as with Samson, His death brought destruction to all of His enemies! All of that being said, what's the significance of Samson and the jawbone? Allow me to ask this question. What IF the donkey represents the Law? Balaam bucked against it. It would not allow his perverse ways to pass. The 'Law' spoke and set Balaam back on track, forcing him to repent even if he got a limp in the process. The Law was used by Samson for the destruction of the enemies of Israel. From wielding it, Samson became thirsty. Therefore through the Law came water which revived Samson's spirit. The place was named Fountain of the Praying One. Does any of this sound like Jesus, our Fountain of Living Water? Does this go any further?

ZEC 9:9 MKJV

(9) Rejoice greatly, O daughter of Zion; shout, O daughter of Jerusalem; behold, your King comes to you. He is righteous and victorious, meek and riding on an ass, even on a colt, the son of an ass.

Jesus fulfilled this scripture by riding into Jerusalem on a donkey. The people celebrated the fulfillment of Zechariah's prophecy by waving palm branches and shouting "Hosanna!" But does it make any sense? Does it make sense, contextually, that the Messiah – Savior of the world – should ride upon the Law of Moses? After all, Paul told us that the Law could only get us so far.

ROM 3:20-23 MKJV

(20) Because by the works of the Law none of all flesh will be justified in His sight; for through the Law is the knowledge of sin.

(21) But now a righteousness of God has been revealed apart from Law, being witnessed by the Law and the Prophets;

(22) even the righteousness of God through the faith of Jesus Christ, toward all and upon all those who believe. For there is no difference,

(23) for all have sinned and come short of the glory of God,

There was no justification in the Law for anyone; therefore there *was* a need for Jesus to satisfy the Law's requirement. Hmmm... let's try to illustrate it one more time.

90

Luk 10:33-34 MKJV

(33) But a certain traveling Samaritan came upon him, and seeing him, he was filled with pity.

(34) And coming near, he bound up his wounds, pouring on oil and wine, and set him on his own animal and brought him to an inn, and took care of him.

In His parable of the Good Samaritan, Jesus talks about a 'savior' who comes along and binds the wounds of the victimized man. After this, He sets the man upon his 'own animal' – read DONKEY, because that is typically what you would see. He then took the man to an inn and left him for two days. The 'Law' will take you so far. In this analogy, the law took the wounded man to a safe place where he was deposited with a down payment from the savior. We could definitely go further, but you can clearly see where following the rabbit has taken me.

Rabbit trails are probably my favorite way to study. My faith tells me that it doesn't matter which way I take, He is able to lead me back to any conclusion He likes. The Word is a fabric, or maybe a net, all woven together. If you have the desire, there is always a way to make point A connect to point B. Typically, my rabbit trails take me to a place that I was not expecting, leaving me scratching my head as to why the Spirit brought me to where He did. But more often than not, within a few days, He will bring me back to that same place – arriving from a different direction. Sometimes it's something a buddy brings up during a lunch break. Sometimes it is the message that is presented in church on Sunday morning. When that happens, I nod to myself, knowing the Holy Spirit wanted to call my name – twice.

TRANSLATIONS
AND SOURCES

People get hung up very often on translations. There are many. The main question is which translation is best? Choose one that is respectful of the text, and that makes sense when you read it. The NIV is written at an 8th grade reading level, and is for that reason not cumbersome. From a scholarship angle, some avoid the NIV because it, like other translations, leaves out some verses that were not found in all manuscripts (even though most NIV's I have seen do include the missing verses in the footnotes).

TRANSLATION METHODS

Truly, the main hurdle in producing a bible translation is not the text itself, but rather the method that the text is translated. There are three basic methods of translation: literal, dynamic equivalency, and paraphrase. Literal translations take a word for word approach to translating the scriptures. I prefer this type of translation, personally, although I will admit it has some inherent flaws. For one, the Hebrew language has some words for which there is no English substitute. What then? Well, that is up to the person that is doing the translating – and that can be problematic because it becomes a matter of interpretation! Dynamic equivalency is a method of taking the text, determining the 'thought' that is being conveyed in context, and writing that thought down. This is perhaps the most controversial method that is used because it effectively puts the translator into the interpretation business. That is a dangerous undertaking. The paraphrase method is when the translator takes the sometimes-archaic working of scripture and simply writes it in his or her own words. This method is 'okay', as long as the translator does not veer from translation into interpretation.

My advice is to have access to as many translations as possible and compare them when studying specific subjects. As I said before, good bible study software will aid in comparisons. We will look at a couple of instances where translational issues might arise, and who it might have the most impact on. As we have already discussed, the Bible is much like a hologram. A hologram is a three dimensional image that is formed by the interference of light beams most-often created with a laser. When we lose a single angle of light in a hologram, we still have the big picture although we do tend to lose a little resolution. If the Gospel of Mark was removed, we would still have three gospels left in which to paint a very detailed picture. Don't rely upon a translation that takes too many liberties with Biblical imagery. For instance… this is one of my favorites (not really, I am being sarcastic). The Holman Christian Standard has this to say about Noah:

GEN 6:9 HCSB

9 These are the family records of Noah. Noah was a righteous man, blameless among his contemporaries; Noah walked with God.

If one meditates on this, it doesn't take long before something starts to smell. *Should* Noah be blameless amongst a world of evil people that the Lord is about to destroy? Is the picture you're getting of a multitude of people robbing, persecuting, and killing one another – all except for Noah, because he was such a swell guy? My guess is that something was lost in translation. A better choice of words that is used at times is 'blameless in his time'. It's easy to see the connection between that phrase and the word 'contemporaries', but one is more sensible. Let's take another look:

GEN 6:9 MKJV

(9) These are the generations of Noah. Noah was a just man and perfect in his generations. Noah walked with God.

This still may not be clear, but at least it's not obviously misleading. At the very least, it makes us wonder – what does it mean to be 'perfect in our generations'? Good question! As it turns out, the Hebrew language sheds great light on this! Without getting into a large discussion about Noah, which really is not the point, I will say that the writers that analyzed the Word in an effort to make the Holman Christian Standard more understandable simply missed a few opportunities to really make us think. This is the biggest problem I see with translational issues: the translator wants to increase readability at the expense of good scholarship. Where words and phrases in the Hebrew or Greek are questioned, many times the final translation leaves nothing for the reader to be suspicious of. If the original Hebrew shows us a word like a'rar (bush with poisonous fruit), our poor translators choose a word like 'heath' (see the verse below) or 'juniper' (Jer 17:6) because it's the closest English equivalent we have to describe such an object.

JER 17:6 KJV

(6) For he shall be like the heath in the desert, and shall not see when good cometh; but shall inhabit the parched places in the wilderness, in a salt land and not inhabited.

What a shame! I'm still waiting on a translation that leaves questionable words and phrases for which we have no English equivalent in their native, transliterated forms. In this way, we would be motivated to research for ourselves any unknown definitions. This is the heart of digging for nuggets! Alas, if there is such a translation, I have not yet found it. Therefore, we must train the eye to be suspicious!

Also, know that some people refer to a paraphrase such as The Message, as a translation. In my own opinion a paraphrase may have its place in your studies, although I would not lean upon this as your main resource. The Message might not accurately depict every scenario found within scripture, but there are times when it sheds light on some very cryptic passages. I know many who stay away from paraphrased Bibles altogether. For those who wish to stay with a fairly accurate translation but steer clear of paraphrases, I would recommend the Amplified Bible. The Amplified is a good study translation because the text is very wordy. Every possibility to elaborate or fully explain a phrase is taken, making it a lot more to read, but much more understandable.

Then we have the crowd that will only adhere to the 1611 King James Version, which was the first mass-produced English version of the text. Being the first, those who are proponents of this version assume that it has fewer translational errors or omissions and is therefore 'the Word' as it was meant to be. Certainly, it is a good translation if you do not mind all of the thee's and thou's. But even this great translation is ineffective in giving us a good feel for scriptural meanings. Let me give you an example. The following passage is taken from the 1611 King James Version:

JOHN 1:29 KJV-1611

(29) The next day, Iohn seeth Iesus comming vnto him, and saith, Behold the Lambe of God, which taketh away the sinne of the world.

Wow… that is different isn't it. All of the "J"s are "I"s! That is truly the King's English. But it's too flowery. In reality, looking at the Greek text, here is what John said:

JOHN 1:29 (COMPLETE JEWISH BIBLE)

(29) The next day, Yochanan saw Yeshua coming toward him and said, "Look! God's lamb! The one who is taking away the sin of the world!

Do you see how raw and earthy that is? This really appeals to me much more. Limiting yourself to only one translation certainly can hinder your understanding. Beyond all of this, I will say that I learned very much from watching my girls' *Read and Share Bible* movies, which were simple bible stories that were retold using animation and voice-overs. These little movies were made for toddlers! But the truths of these are just as heavy and relevant as ever and I see new applications every time I see them. The Holy Spirit will teach you through His word!

WHAT ABOUT CHRONOLOGICAL BIBLES?

Chronological Bibles have gotten very popular in the last decade. Many churches have instituted programs of reading the Bible through in a year with their congregations, which is a productive thing to do. There is no penalty for reading the books out of order! Discovering the true chronology of biblical events is highly interesting and I would recommend that everyone try reading the bible through in this way at least once. But there are a couple of issues to be aware of when reading the bible on a schedule. The biggest problem is that when we do anything on a schedule, the tendency is to miss the leading of the Spirit. When I'm tired after a long day, or feeling sick, yet I feel I must read the book of Joel tonight because I cannot get off schedule, then what are the chances I am really going to get anything out of Joel's work? Not good. The double edge to this is supposing I feel sick... I do decide to take it easy and pretty soon I'm five days or a week behind and all of a sudden the enemy is giving me the guilt trip because I couldn't keep up. That is empty religion at its finest! Avoid it!

STUDY BIBLES

Study bibles can be great because the individual who compiles it (typically in an existing version) will add his or her study notes in the margins. It's a great way to learn from some smart and gifted folks for sure! What we are actually doing, usually, is adding a commentary to the Word, which is fine as long as we all realize… it is what it is. It is a scholar's take or opinion on scripture. It may be right, or not. If you do purchase a study bible, try to get one that is compiled by a trusted, God-hungry man or woman who has an anointed ministry to teach.

There are also some neat study bibles available that employ pictures much like an encyclopedia. To me, these are very enjoyable because I have a constant visual prop in the margin. Many of these will show pictures of ancient farm implements, diagrams of hideouts, or maps of places that no longer exist. These all serve to help me remember what I read.

EXTRA-BIBLICAL SOURCES

Extra-biblical Sources can really aid in your search for knowledge or clarity. Unfortunately, these sources can pose some dangers to those who one, do not know what the Bible says about a subject already, or two, do not know how to find out! Sources are great. I am not one of those who ascribe to the belief that we should never use extra-biblical sources for study. I do have the Holy Spirit in me that can guide me in all truth. I am not threatened by any resource that I might find or that someone might give me. If it contains materials that contradict what the Bible says, His Spirit lets me know. That's all well-and-good, Steve, but what if I'm not as familiar with scripture? I'm glad you asked!

Let me get very fundamental here. If you are seeking teaching on signs, wonders, and miracles, you probably will not find a lot of materials in your local Baptist bookstore. This is because most Baptist doctrines do not focus on signs, wonders, and miracles and that particular denomination monitors carefully the products that grace their shelves. If they do have materials on signs, wonders, and miracles, they will probably be based upon a strictly Baptist denominational viewpoint. All denominations tend to do this, and should not be a surprise to anyone at all! I go to the Baptist bookstore all the time, but not for books on signs, wonders, and miracles necessarily. Go to a non-denominational bookstore where all types of books are on the shelves in order to find information on subject matter that spans all types of denominations, or that does not deal with any specific denominational doctrine. Oh, and just because we find interesting materials at a non-denominational bookstore doesn't mean it is truth, either. It simply means there was no governing body that prevented the book to be sold at that store! Incidentally, the largest non-denominational bookstore that I know of is the internet!

Perhaps the best way to obtain obscure study material is to find someone whom you respect greatly in the faith and ask them to recommend books for you. You will likely find a series of books by one or two authors, and by reading those you will also discover the resources used by *those* authors… and so on. Do not be afraid to read a book! But if you do not know if a statement made by an author is truthful, underline it and have someone help you research it in scriptures. This will be a tremendous learning tool in itself!

HISTORY BOOKS – CAN THEY BE TRUSTED?

Some people love to read old history books in conjunction with their study of scriptures. Fantastic! Me too! The question always comes up, though. Can we trust our history books? Yes absolutely, but, not all the time! History books are typically recorded by people who have gathered information – to the best of their ability – and compiled it all into a book. Does it mean it is all correct? No, certainly not. But you can bet that a great portion of it is truthful as long as the book was not created with an agenda in mind. This can be the case for modern history and text books, especially, where we all know that the writer may have a political or religious agenda pushing him or her to omit or include certain information. Again, the ultimate test for the information we glean in our extrabiblical studies is this: does the information agree with what is written in the Word? If the Word is silent on a subject, is it possible that it could accommodate what the history book says?

For instance, Jewish history states that during the time of Jesus, there was little wood available for building fires. Everyone needed fire to warm their homes and cook on, so what did they use? They used the only resource they had in complete abundance. Animal dung! This did a couple of things. It prevented a pileup of animal dung around the house (good, as there was usually a shortage of Febreze also), and it prevented the need to gather wood which was in short supply. History also states that if the people were to take salt and mix it with the dung, it would burn hotter, longer. Cool! So what? If the salt were no longer good, it was dug out of the fire pit and thrown out into the street.

MAT 5:13 MKJV

(13) You are the salt of the earth, but if the salt loses its savor, with what shall it be salted? It is no longer good for anything, but to be thrown out and to be trodden underfoot by men.

Now for me, I tend to associate "savor" with "flavor", and that is not necessarily a good association. In the Greek, savor can also mean 'potency'. This is valuable historical information, because I see that part of our 'job' as the salt of the earth is to make others burn hotter, and burn longer. This is the type of information I tend to glean most frequently from history books.

Some history books tackle subjects like "Did the Philistines Really Exist"? I don't waste my time reading anything that approaches a biblical subject from the angle of unbelief. This is a matter of stewardship of my time to me. I always have a choice to make of whether I wish to spend my energy examining good, faith-filled scholarship, or a skeptical secular view where I always end up spitting out mostly bones and getting very little meat.

LISTEN

JER 23:18 MKJV

(18) For who has stood in the counsel of Jehovah, and hears His Word? Who has listened to His Word and heard it?

LISTENING FOR REVELATION

The people in Jesus' day marveled about how He learned the Word. Contrary to what scripture says about Jesus, many believe He just knew the Word because He was the Word (John 1)! That's just not so! The prophet Isaiah had insight as to how the Messiah would learn:

ISA 50:4-5 MKJV

(4) The Lord Jehovah has given Me the tongue of the learned, to know to help the weary with a word. He wakens morning by morning, He wakens the ear to hear as the learned.

(5) The Lord Jehovah has opened My ear, and I was not rebellious, nor turned away backwards.

Jesus was awakened in the morning listening to God! He learned from God Himself, as God had given Him ears to hear. In the Revelation of Jesus, Jesus says multiple times, "He who has an ear, let him hear what the Spirit says." Many, many times in scripture the phrase "bowing the ear" is used. Bowing the ear does not simply mean hearing, but it means listening receptively, or receiving. It is a matter of the heart. When we strongly desire to receive a word from God, He often will grant us the word because we 'have an ear to hear' it – even if we are asleep!

JOB 4:12-14 MKJV

(12) And a word was secretly brought to me, and my ear received a little of it.

(13) In thoughts from the visions of the night, when deep sleep falls upon men,

(14) fear came upon me, and trembling, which made all my bones shake.

Job received bits and pieces of revelation from God while he slept. It was not a word he really desired, but God knew he had a receptive heart. At times God may use such a dream or vision to reinforce something we have been contemplating.

JOB 33:15-16 MKJV

(15) In a dream, a vision of the night, when deep sleep falls on men; while they slumber on the bed;

(16) then He opens the ear of men and seals their teaching,

David said it this way:

PSA 16:7 MKJV

(7)   I will bless Jehovah, who has given me wisdom; my heart also instructs me in the nights.

The Apostle Paul (Saul before his conversion) was one of the brightest minds of his day. He had been trained by Gamaliel, which would be much akin to saying you had been tutored by Albert Einstein. He was in the "who's-who" of religious minds of Jesus' day. But when Paul came to know Jesus personally through his vision, he realized just how much he did not know. Who did he turn to?

GAL 1:15-18 MKJV

(15)   But when it pleased God, who separated me from my mother's womb, and having called me by His grace,

(16)   to reveal His Son in me so that I might preach Him among the nations, immediately I did not confer with flesh and blood;

(17)   Nor did I go up to Jerusalem to those apostles before me, but I went into Arabia and returned again to Damascus.

(18)   Then after three years I went up to Jerusalem to see Peter, and stayed with him fifteen days.

Paul turned only to God Himself! He went to the desert of Arabia where he listened and meditated for three years. The only scripture he had to that point was the Torah and the writings of the prophets, which he had undoubtedly memorized. With this knowledge he went camping and returned with a personal relationship with the Author.

THE ZEALOUS PRACTICE OF MEDITATION

Listening, or meditating, is much more difficult to learn than it seems. Meditation is a stilling of the flesh so that the spirit can hear. It requires purpose and focus. Most of us have busy lives with our occupations and our families. If you have tried meditation, you know that it is a challenge to sit quietly for any length of time and not fall asleep! But if God is able to teach us while we sleep, then what is the point of wasting time with conscious meditation? First of all, we are instructed to meditate:

JOS 1:8 MKJV

(8) This book of the Law shall not depart out of your mouth, but you shall meditate on it by day and by night, so that you may be careful to do according to all that is written in it. For then you shall make your way prosperous, and then you shall act wisely.

Let's take a deeper look at what God means by 'meditation'. I'm going to chase a rabbit here, so hang with me.

ISA 31:4 MKJV

(4) For so has Jehovah spoken to me: As the lion roars, even the young lion on his prey when a multitude of shepherds are gathered against him, he will not be afraid of their voice, nor fret himself because of their noise. So Jehovah of Hosts shall come down to fight for Mount Zion, and on its hill.

The Hebrew word here for 'roars', or 'roaring' in the King James is 'haggah'. Study this verse carefully. We've all seen a dog chewing on a bone, knowing full-well that to attempt to take the bone from him might cost us a hand or a finger. This is what 'haggah' means. It also means 'to meditate'! God means for us to meditate in such a way that we consume, utterly, and with such zeal that nobody or nothing would even entertain the notion of distracting us from what we are pondering. This is a powerful concept! It is probably a way to view meditation that you have never considered! The psalmist uses the idea here:

PSA 1:1-2 MKJV

> (1) Blessed is the man who has not walked in the counsel of the ungodly, and has not stood in the way of sinners, and has not sat in the seat of the scornful.

> (2) But his delight is only in the Law of Jehovah; and in His Law he meditates day and night.

Yes, this underlined portion is 'haggah'! It even sounds like a roar, in a way! Consume what you meditate upon!

Secondly, our intellect can get in the way of our spiritual understanding. Meditation can help us to pound our intellect into submission! New Age mysticism has stolen this idea from the Holy Spirit and has twisted it into something so hideous that Christians are often afraid to consider it. On the other hand, it is my belief that the danger of New Age meditation is that it operates according to the desires of the enemy, which is for us to be 'empty', spiritually. This is supposedly in order to make room for truth or enlightenment. The problem with this tenet is that there is room in your house (your body) for more than one spirit! If you are not full of the Holy Spirit, then emptying your house may make room for spirits that you don't want (Matt 12:45)!

HEARING WITH SPIRITUAL EARS

1COR 14:14 MKJV

> (14) For if I pray in a tongue, my spirit prays, but my mind is unfruitful.

Paul teaches us that the mind and spirit are not usually on the same wavelength! There are some things God desires to teach us in the spirit without us having to wrestle intellectually with the concept. In fact, so much of what God has to teach us is just flat-out offensive to our mind. My mentor often says that the mind makes a great servant, but a horrible master! So true this is! To illustrate, Jesus told a crowd of people, "Unless you eat the flesh of the Son of Man, and drink His blood, you do not have life in yourselves" (John 6:54). This is spiritual truth, but to our intellect, it's offensive! It certainly turned off many of the Jewish listeners in the crowd who wandered away murmuring against Jesus. Why would Jesus do this? Did He not realize that He was speaking to a group of people who believed what Torah said about drinking blood? It was an abomination (Gen 9:4, Lev 17:14)! Jesus taught us through this act that enduring the offense of the flesh is often what is necessary to climb further-up and further-into the Spirit. When the flesh is offended, look for a doorway to the staircase leading up. What you hear with your flesh may not be the same as what you hear with your spirit. It is a battle, and that which is stronger will likely win. Meditation is one way to test an offensive word.

Most of us have heard it said, "I just knew in my heart it was going to happen!" Whatever 'it' was… we realize there is an instinct, or an inner knowledge that often supersedes any head-knowledge we might have. Mothers and fathers tend to have a spiritual connection to their children. This is why listening and meditation are so important. It provides the time necessary for the mind to release and the spirit to process what was said.

To hear from God and do what He instructs is our goal. Jesus did some strange things! Yet, He told us that He only did what He saw the Father doing, and spoke what the Father taught! (John 5:19, 8:28) Looking at the way Jesus ministered to people, if we do not take into account His ability to hear from God, we are bound to be puzzled by why He did things as He did.

MAR 7:32-35 MKJV

(32) And they brought a deaf one to Him, hardly speaking. And they begged Him to put His hand on him.

(33) And He took him aside from the crowd and put His fingers into his ears. And He spat and touched his tongue.

(34) And looking up to Heaven, He sighed and said to him, Ephphatha! (that is, Be opened!)

(35) And instantly his ears were opened and the bond of his tongue was loosened, and he spoke plainly.

Many of us attend churches where our elders regularly pray for healing as the Bible instructs... At times, even, we might attend a healing service somewhere. How many times do we see something occur like what Jesus did in order to heal the deaf man? I'd wager that in our culture, if we attempt to heal in this manner we would get slapped with a lawsuit! If Jesus only did what He saw His Father doing... and He operated solely from listening to the Spirit, then that tells me more about my ability to listen than it does my ability to heal. Could it be that my anointing to heal is directly related to my ability to listen?

FAITH BUILDING

Listening will help you build your faith!

Rom 10:17 MKJV

(17) Then faith is of hearing, and hearing by the Word of God.

That's right! Faith comes by hearing. We often hear "I'll believe it when I see it!" Not true! So many people who saw the miracles of Jesus (including His close followers) did not believe Him to be who He said He was. David wrote in the Psalms, "Be still and know that I am God." Being still is the heart of the idea of listening. What might we gather from David's experience of being still? Do you think perhaps his early days of watching his sheep pick over the barren grounds of the desert provided him the time to learn the discipline of stillness? As the sun set, no doubt he sat perched upon a rock, strumming his lyre and voicing his praises to God. Maybe it was his endless hours of practicing with his sling-shot, as Bedouin boys do. Yes, David had quiet time, and it allowed him to know God intimately so that when the giants came, he was not alarmed. He had already seen beyond the giant! God had shown him his destiny in his stillness, and he had no fear!

God desires our ears. If faith comes by hearing, and we cannot please God without faith, then it's God's deep desire that we learn to listen when He speaks. To the contrary, this is not unknown to the enemy, who would constantly provide either noise or antago-nistic voices for us to key on. Yes, the devil wants to tie up your ears. In the computer industry, this is known as a 'denial of serv-ice' attack. A cyber criminal will send so much traffic to a website that nobody else can get on that website. The devil does 'denial of service' attacks to people every day. It's one of his favorite strate-gies to keep our ears occupied!

ACT 16:16-18 MKJV

(16) And as we went to prayer, it happened that a cer-tain girl possessed with a spirit of divination met us, who brought her masters much gain by divining.

(17) The same followed Paul and us and cried, saying, These men are the servants of the Most High God, who are announcing to us the way of salvation.

(18) And she did this many days. But being distressed, and turning to the demonic spirit, Paul said, I command you in the name of Jesus Christ to come out of her! And it came out in that hour.

This passage has confused many a reader. After all, why would a demon tell the truth? Why would this even be a problem? The answer is that a spirit of divination (or Phythonic spirit, in the

LITV) acts just like a denial of service attack. The spirit constantly spouts out noise that ultimately is a distraction to the real message that needs to be spoken – the Gospel. The python squeezes its prey until it is dead from lack of oxygen. The spirit of Python squeezes its victim so that no air of truth can get in. This is how badly the devil wants to keep you from listening!

DISCERNING HIS VOICE

Jesus said, "My sheep hear my voice, and I know them, and they follow me" (John 10:27). This is both a source of security and consternation to Christians. Many of us have never been taught how to listen and discern the voice of God. Therefore, worry and doubt creep in because we wonder if we are truly His sheep, acknowledging our inability to hear Him speak. I'd like to shed some light on this.

Let's take a look at the difference between how those who know Him hear His voice, and how those that do not know Him hear his voice. Two instances readily come to mind in scripture where there was this (modernized) proclamation: "Wow! This really IS the Son of God!" The first is made by those who were close to Jesus and were in the dead center of a storm:

MAT 14:32-33 MKJV

> (32) And when they had come into the boat, the wind ceased.

> (33) And those in the boat came and worshiped Him, saying, Truly You are the Son of God.

It's usually a "duh" moment when the Prince of Peace brings peace to a storm in our life. Seriously though, what else would He do? Well, that depends on who you ask. The world has a different perception of God and what He brings.

MAT 27:54 MKJV

(54) But the centurion and those guarding Jesus, seeing the earthquake, and the things that took place, they feared greatly, saying, Truly this One was Son of God.

Is it not a little strange that those who do not know God see Him as a violent force, out to destroy anyone smaller than He is (which, I guess is just about everyone)? If you know God, then you recognize peace as what He brings. If you do not know God, then you believe destruction and chaos is His signature. Elijah experienced this very differentiation!

1KI 19:11-12 MKJV

(11) And He said, Go forth and stand on the mountain before Jehovah. And, behold, Jehovah passed by, and a great and strong wind tore the mountains, and broke the rocks in pieces before Jehovah. But Jehovah was not in the wind. And after the wind was an earthquake, but Jehovah was not in the earthquake.

(12) And after the earthquake was a fire, but Jehovah was not in the fire. And after the fire was a still, small voice.

If you are aching to hear His voice when you listen for Him and you are concerned that you do not hear audible words, I would ask the question: do you feel peace? His peace is one way He communicates with His sheep! Even if we have been in rebellion, God deals gently with us. Paul provides us with another perfect example of this! As he was traveling down the road to Damascus, he is knocked down on the road and blinded by a bright light. Now, that might not seem too gentle, but it certainly was not fire and brimstone. In fact, notice how God speaks to Paul!

ACT 9:4-5 MKJV

(4) And he fell to the earth and heard a voice saying to him, Saul, Saul, why do you persecute Me?

(5) And he said, Who are you, lord? And the Lord said, I am Jesus whom you persecute. It is hard for you to kick against the goads.

Saul was on his way to murder more Christians because – honestly – he believed this was God's will. Saul was zealous for God! This might be surprising to consider, but God hints at this by what He tells Saul: "It is hard for you to kick against the goads." A goad is what a shepherd uses to keep his cattle or flock in line – it's a prod, of sorts. Why would God use such an instrument if Saul was not a part of the flock, even if a rebellious part?

There are times when we know, without a doubt, that God speaks to us. He speaks by His own (still small) voice, through His word, through others around us, and through the peace in our own heart. Even so, there are times when we do not hear what the Shepherd says. Look up. Are there other sheep near? Then yes, you are still in the herd and all is okay. When in doubt of what the Shepherd said, simply follow the sheep next to you who is listening. This is how sheep are designed. If you do not see any sheep near, sit tight. The Shepherd is coming for you (Luke 15:4)!

GOD'S TIMING

There is yet another aspect of listening that we should consider. If we are able to hear what the Holy Spirit tells us in regard to instruction for our lives and ministry, then our timing will be perfect! Just because scripture tells us it is legal to do something, if we do not know when to do it the results may not be great. Paul said it like this:

1Co 6:12a All things are lawful to me, but not all things profit

Paul knew the great commission as well as anyone, and he knew his calling was to preach the Gospel to the nations.

GAL 1:15-16 MKJV

(15) But when it pleased God, who separated me from my mother's womb, and having called me by His grace,

(16) to reveal His Son in me so that I might preach Him among the nations, immediately I did not confer with flesh and blood;

It says here that Paul did not confer with flesh and blood, but with the Spirit! Because he did this, he also knew that just because his calling was to share the gospel to the nations, it did not mean that he could just pick a spot and start preaching!

ACT 16:6 MKJV

(6) And coming through the Phrygian and the Galatian region; and by the Holy Spirit being forbidden to speak the Word in Asia;

The Spirit forbade him to go to Asia. Why is this? Ultimately, we don't know, but what we do know is that if we cannot hear from the Holy Spirit, we may find ourselves in a spot we may have never been destined for. A bad spot, at that!

Listening and meditating on the Word is probably the most understated method of coming into a real understanding of Truth. That is because Truth is a person, and one cannot simply understand who He is without knowing Him intimately. I've read the biography of C.S. Lewis, and try as I may, even if I memorize it, I will not obtain an understanding of the man in comparison to that of his own son. There is no substitute for personal relationship. There are many who can stand up on Sunday and read scriptures. There are slightly fewer who can give a surface explanation of those scriptures. But a deep understanding of the ways of God requires sitting at His feet, being silent, and listening.

MORE HOLLOW TILES

Perhaps you just read this famous verse:

DEU 8:3 MKJV

(3) And He humbled you and allowed you to hunger, and then He fed you with manna, which you did not know, neither did your fathers know it, so that He might make you know that man shall not live by bread alone, but by every word that comes out of the mouth of Jehovah man shall live.

Man shall not live by bread alone. In meditating on this verse, I found that phrase jumped out at me. If I rephrased it to "Man shall not fish by boat alone", then my mind would immediately ask the question: what else, then, do I need to fish? Obviously, in the case of fishing, there are many things one needs to fish other than a boat, unless your name is Gollum.

When God says, "Man shall not live by bread alone, but by…" I realize He is about to let me in on a secret. It is here that I will mention something else about the text and how it is written. In most translations, if the word or phrase is italicized, then it is not found in the original manuscript, but rather is added by the translator in order to make the statement make sense.

DEU 8:3 MKJV

(3) And He humbled you and allowed you to hunger, and then He fed you with manna, which you did not know, neither did your fathers know it, so that He might make you know that man shall not live by bread alone, but by every word that comes out of the mouth of Jehovah man shall live.

This verse has a very conspicuous word in italics: word. So if we remove it and read it as the original text reads, it looks like this:

DEU 8:3 MKJV

(3) And He humbled you and allowed you to hunger, and then He fed you with manna, which you did not know, neither did your fathers know, so that He might make you know that man shall not live by bread alone, but by every that comes out of the mouth of Jehovah man shall live.

That makes absolutely no sense! The translators did a good job here. First of all, why is there no noun in that phrase? How can that make sense in any language? In our chapter The Jewish Angle, we discussed the remez, which is a purposeful exclusion in order to hint at a truth. This reminds me of just that! The noun is omitted and instead we have the Hebrew phrase, "that comes out of", which is synonymous with the English term "issuance". The verse would then read:

DEU 8:3 MKJV

(3) And He humbled you and allowed you to hunger, and then He fed you with manna, which you did not know, neither did your fathers know it, so that He might make you know that man shall not live by bread alone, but by every issuance from the mouth of Jehovah man shall live.

That is an odd phrase. Again, I think we've just rolled our desk chair over a hollow tile in the floor. There's more to this than meets the eye! Now, from my perspective, I simply must ask the question. When I'm reading the scriptures and they tell me that man does not live by bread alone, then what or whom must also be necessary for living? My immediate response: Jesus! After all, we are reading scripture here! Let us take a quick look at the Hebrew phrase 'issuance from'. The word is 'matzah'. If you are Jewish, you will recognize this term as a type of 'bread' used primarily in the Passover meal. Has Jesus ever referred to Himself as 'bread'? He was born in Bethlehem, which means 'house of bread'. Here we begin to see the power of the Hebrew language. Matzah literally means source, dawn, rising of the sun, gate, fountain, bud, that which came out, outgoing, or springs. Jesus said,

- If you had asked of Him, He would have given you **living water** (John 4:10)
- The water which I will give to him will become a **fountain** (John 4:14)
- I am the **door** (gate; John 10:7)
- I will lead them to **springs** (Rev 7:17)

The bud is also a Jesus reference, as the staff of Aaron budded – bringing life out of something dead. The rising of the sun (son) is also a reference to the Messiah that we find in the Old Testament scriptures. It is now easy to see that this entire scripture reference is about Jesus, hidden in the Hebrew language and to God's very word to His people. To add depth, we might ask how man came to 'live' in the first place.

GEN 2:7 MKJV

(7) And Jehovah God formed man of the dust of the ground, and breathed into his nostrils the breath of life; and man became a living soul.

It sounds as though everything that *issues from the mouth of God* gives life to man, truly! Does it remind you at all of this verse?

Joh 20:22 MKJV

(22) And when He had said this, He breathed on them and said to them, Receive the Holy Spirit.

What is God saying again? Everything that HE breathes gives life.

CLUELESS

Sometimes I read a story and even if I enjoy it, I simply have no clue about what it means. Let me give you one of my favorite examples of this. It's the story of Balaam. Now Balaam is a HUGE study of a man that seems intent on doing it all wrong. He hears from God, truly enough. Yet he makes it his life work to promote himself, being a prophetic mercenary for hire rather than a messenger for God.

Num 22:20-33 MKJV

(20) And God came to Balaam at night and said to him, If the men come to call you, rise up, go with them. But still, the word which I shall say to you, that you shall do.

(21) And Balaam rose up in the morning and saddled his ass, and went with the rulers of Moab.

(22) And God's anger was kindled because he went. And the Angel of Jehovah stood in the way as an enemy against him. And he was riding upon his ass, and his two servants with him.

(23) And the ass saw the Angel of Jehovah standing in the way, and His sword drawn in His hand. And the ass turned aside out of the way and went into the field. And Balaam struck the ass, to turn her into the way.

(24) But the Angel of Jehovah stood in a path of the vine-yards, a wall on this side, and a wall on that side.

(25) And when the ass saw the Angel of Jehovah, she pushed herself into the wall and crushed Balaam's foot against the wall. And he struck her again.

(26) And the Angel of Jehovah went further and stood in a narrow place, where there was no way to turn either to the right hand or to the left.

(27) And when the ass saw the Angel of Jehovah, she fell down under Balaam. And Balaam's anger was kindled, and he struck the ass with a staff.

(28) And Jehovah opened the mouth of the ass, and she said to Balaam, What have I done to you, that you have beaten me these three times?

(29) And Balaam said to the ass, Because you have mocked me. I wish there were a sword in my hand, for now I would kill you.

(30) And the ass said to Balaam, Am I not your ass, upon which you have ridden ever since I was yours, to this day? Was I ever known to do so to you? And he said, No.

(31) Then Jehovah opened the eyes of Balaam, and he saw the Angel of Jehovah standing in the way, and His sword drawn in His hand. And he bowed down his head, and fell on his face.

(32) And the Angel of Jehovah said to him, Why have you beaten your ass these three times? Behold! I went out to be an enemy to you, because your way is perverse before Me.

(33) And the ass saw Me and turned from Me these three times. Unless she had turned from Me, surely now I also would have killed you and saved her alive.

To start with, this is a difficult story to tell to an American audience because of the wording. It's hard not to chuckle at the story of Balaam getting his foot crushed by an obstinate donkey, but when we go with the original translation of 'ass', things can get downright amusing. Even so, this story starts with a mystery. God told Balaam to go with the leaders of Moab, who wanted to bring him to Balak, the king, for the purpose of cursing Israel. So immediately in verse 21 we see that he does go with the officials, and God's anger was kindled against him. Why? Was he not doing exactly what God instructed? It's a humorous episode, but what exactly does it have to do with anything?

There is a clue in this story about why God is so angry with Balaam. In verse 32, we see that the Angel tells him that his way is perverse. That means it is twisted, or two-faced. Balaam wanted to hear from God, but serve the enemy. How so?

We see that the wicked Moabite king, Balak, tried three times to get Balaam to curse Israel because he was afraid of their prosperity and large numbers of people. Each time, Balaam entertained Balak's request and approached God, who promptly told him that cursing Israel was not an option because He had blessed Israel.

NUM 24:10 MKJV

(10) And Balak's anger was kindled against Balaam. And he struck his hands together. And Balak said to Balaam, I called you to curse my enemies, and behold, you have kept on blessing these three times.

You might think that one conversation with God on that issue would be enough. Not so. Balaam did it three times! Not once did God let Balaam have any leeway with Balak. Why was Balaam so persistent? Most likely he was looking for something from God that would allow him a paycheck from Balak. Nehemiah described it this way:

NEH 13:1-2 MKJV

(1) On that day they read in the book of Moses in the ears of the people. And in it was found written that the Ammonite and the Moabite should not come into the congregation of God forever,

(2) because they did not meet the sons of Israel with bread and with water, but hired Balaam against them so that he should curse them. But our God turned the curse into a blessing.

Three times Balaam attempted to curse Israel and earn his paycheck. Three times God said "No". Three times Balaam attempted to move forward on his donkey, and three times was he blocked by God. What was the result of this persistent movement against the will of God? For one, Balaam got his foot crushed. When we continually clash against the will of God, we develop a spiritual limp. In fact, it's possible it can give us a permanent limp. Such was what happened to Balaam. He never recovered from trying to curse Israel. The act seared his conscience to the point where he continued to live with the enemy while believing himself to be righteous. God did use his gifting, but in the end it led to his own destruction, much like Samson. When Israel later invaded the land of Midian, they also killed Balaam, who was dwelling there.

What can we learn from this story? It is abundantly clear that if God blesses, there is no way to curse. Oh my! What are the implications of that? If we are children of God, are we blessed? If we are blessed, can we be cursed? This story indicates that to be impossibility! Then how does so much bad stuff seem to happen to blessed people? Good question! What did Balaam do when he could not curse Israel? He did exactly what the devil does to God's children today: he set a trap, causing them to sin. This activates a law that is called the Law of Sowing and Reaping! Per Balaam's instruction, he had Balak throw a festival in which the daughters of Moab danced around in their underwear – and all of the Israelite men were invited. This was an effective trap to get the Israelite men to bow down to the Moabite gods, which in turn forced God's judgment – a plague that killed twenty-four thousand people!

NUM 25:1-3 MKJV

(1) And Israel lived in Shittim, and the people began to fornicate with the daughters of Moab.

(2) And they called the people to the sacrifices of their gods. And the people ate and bowed down to their gods.

(3) And Israel joined himself to Baal-peor. And the anger of Jehovah was kindled against Israel.

In this rather large hollow tile, I went a long time not understanding that there was a connection between the story of Balaam and his donkey, and Balaam's attempted cursing of Israel for Balak. Which story came first? The story of Balaam and his donkey in chapter 22 came first. Very often in scripture, we can see that **a physical story represents a spiritual truth**. This is the case with Balaam. I should have been more aware of the story being used in this way when I saw some very, very out-of-place descriptions being used.

"But the Angel of Jehovah stood in a path of the vineyards"

Did the story ever say that Balaam was heading toward vineyards? No! Then why would scripture provide such detail? Because if we are perverse in our pursuits, we will have no access to the 'wine' of the Holy Spirit. As well, why would such a detail as the donkey crushing Balaam's foot be mentioned? Because when we are perverse in our pursuits, our walk can be severely damaged! I certainly should have kept reading the entire story of Balaam in order to connect all of the dots. The story of Balaam and his donkey is a physical reflection of Balaam's spiritual state. The donkey was far more intelligent than Balaam!

The Skeptic
Plan

Perhaps a better name for this section would be the Skeptic System, but I thought someone might misread it and I would hate to give the wrong impression! I looked up the word 'skeptic'. It's an interesting definition (taken from dictionary.com):

SKEP·TIC (NOUN)

1. a person who questions the validity or authenticity of something purporting to be factual.
2. a person who maintains a doubting attitude, as toward values, plans, statements, or the character of others.
3. a person who doubts the truth of a religion, especially christianity, or of important elements of it.
4. (initial capital letter) Philosophy .
   a. a member of a philosophical school of ancient Greece, the earliest group of which consisted of Pyrrho and his followers, who maintained that real knowledge of things is impossible.

b. any later thinker who doubts or questions the possibility of real knowledge of any kind.

Do you see a pattern amongst the definitions? Every one of them is characterized by doubt. Doubt is the enemy of faith.

MAT 14:31 MKJV

(31) And immediately Jesus stretched out His hand and caught him; and said to him, Little-faith! Why did you doubt?

Regardless of our stance upon studying scriptures – whether from a purely academic standpoint, or for the purpose of drawing closer to God, we must realize that if the scriptures are indeed factual then our attitude towards study will affect how much benefit we derive from it. To approach study from the angle of skepticism is like bowling with one leg. It's not easy!

Skepticism is rooted in pride. The assumption that I make when I am a skeptic is that I know better! In the life of a skeptic, there is never a realization or acknowledgment that what I do not know is every bit as important as what I do know.

DEU 8:3 MKJV

(3) And He humbled you and allowed you to hunger, and then He fed you with manna, which you did not know, neither did your fathers know it, so that He might make you know that man shall not live by bread alone, but by every word that comes out of the mouth of Jehovah man shall live.

As you can tell, I do love this verse! We've studied it previously, but now let's take another look at it. Moses is telling the people that God fed them with manna, which they did not know, and that their fathers did not know, so that He might make them know! Read it carefully! Yes, God uses what we do not know in order to introduce us to something new! In this case, God used manna to show people that He was not limited to what they were familiar with to sustain them. Were the people skeptical? Probably! But hunger has a way of getting us past that type of skepticism.

Can I be *skeptical* about something and be correct? Yes! Can I be *a skeptic* and be correct? No! Skepticism is an improper vantage point that *begins* in unbelief. Do not be confused. We are not to be gullible, but we are to have the faith like a child's. If presented with purported factual information, we can know better (not skeptical) and be correct. Or we can 'think' we know better (skeptical) and be either accidentally correct – or dead wrong. See the difference? Why this important distinction?

MAT 16:1-4 MKJV

(1) The Pharisees and the Sadducees came to Him, tempting Him. And they asked Him that He would show them a sign from Heaven.

(2) He answered and said to them, When it is evening, you say, Fair weather; for the sky is red.

(3) And in the morning, Foul weather today; for the sky is red and gloomy. Hypocrites! You can discern the face of the sky, but you cannot see the signs of the times!

(4) A wicked and adulterous generation seeks after a sign. And there shall no sign be given to it, except the sign of the prophet Jonah. And He left them and went away.

There were multitudes following Jesus around daily when He taught. Many believed every word He said. For them, the miracles and signs He performed simply confirmed His identity to them. But for those who did not believe what He said, the signs and wonders fed a need to be entertained in the flesh. This type of hunger cannot be satiated, and Jesus knew it. For the skeptic, there is no sign given. Is that profound? These people followed Jesus daily and watched His works, yet they asked for a sign. They had missed the fact that Jesus Himself was a walking sign. Although surrounded by signs, none of the signs were for them, and therefore they always wished to see that which they had no capacity to see. You could liken this to a wealthy man starving to death in a stocked grocery store because he has no capacity to detect the food he is surrounded with. Skepticism is dangerous!

PARABLES

Jesus could sense a skeptical mind. He did not have much tolerance towards those who required proof of everything because His message was one that required faith. It was because of the skeptics that Jesus adopted the method of teaching in parables, for parables revealed truth only to those who really sought truth. This, too, confused some of His followers. They inquired about His use of parables.

MAT 13:10-13 MKJV

(10) And the disciples said to Him, Why do You speak to them in parables?

(11) He answered and said to them, Because it is given to you to know the mysteries of the kingdom of Heaven, but it is not given to them.

(12) For whoever has, to him shall be given, and he shall have more abundance. But whoever does not have, from him shall be taken away even that which he has.

(13) Therefore I speak to them in parables, because seeing they see not, and hearing they hear not; nor do they understand.

Why was it given to His disciples to know the mysterious truths that Jesus taught? They were not skeptics (well, at least not all). James 4:6 and 1 Peter 5:5 both claim the same truth (hmmm...

they fulfilled our golden rule, didn't they). God resists the proud. God will not reveal Himself to the heart of a skeptic because the skeptic already "knows better". What a sad place to be! For one last illustration, we might mention Thomas. Thomas doubted to the point that he gained the nickname - doubting Thomas!

Thomas had said, publicly, that he would not believe that Jesus was alive until he could place his fingers into the nail scars of Jesus' hands. Was Thomas skeptical? Yes.

JOH 20:27-28 MKJV

(27) Then He said to Thomas, Reach your finger here and behold My hands; and reach your hand here and thrust it into My side; and do not be unbelieving, but believing.

(28) And Thomas answered and said to Him, My Lord and my God!

Afterwards, we see the response of a broken Thomas. "My Lord and my God!" More so, this is the response of a broken skeptic. Yes, we can be skeptical at times, but we cannot live our lives as a skeptic and expect to grow in revelation of truth.

In order to reveal a more non-skeptical approach to study, let us take a quick look at a group known as the Bereans.

ACT 17:10-11 MKJV

(10) And the brothers immediately sent Paul and Silas away by night to Berea. They, when they arrived, went into the synagogue of the Jews.

(11) And these were more noble than those of Thessalonica, in that they received the Word with all readiness of mind and searched the Scriptures daily to see if those things were so.

The Jews of Berea measured truth by comparing what was said with what was written in order to prove what was said... not in order to disprove. Again, to many this may appear to be the same thing. It's a perspective problem. Never begin in doubt. Always begin with faith!

READING INTO SCRIPTURE MEANING

One of the arguments commonly heard amongst skeptic circles is that anyone can make scriptures say anything they like. Specifically, their complaint is that Christians make the Bible say what they want it to say. I hate to admit it, but it's an accurate statement to a point. Many Christians DO twist scriptures, wrongly dividing them in order to justify a position they maintain. I would also contend that many people use Volkswagen Bugs to pull campers. It's an improper use, and it will eventually come back to haunt them! If I have always been taught that sex and love is the same thing and I am now a heavy proponent of this view, then the story of Jonathan and David might be proof, to me, that the two were in a homosexual relationship. After all, David wrote the following about Jonathan:

2SA 1:26 MKJV

> (26) I am distressed for you, my brother Jonathan. Very pleasant you have been to me. Your love to me was wonderful, more than the love of women.

There it is. That's scriptural proof (to me) that David was in a homosexual relationship with Jonathan. Do you see how easy it might be to use scripture to improperly justify an agenda-driven idea? This is commonly the case with opponents of Christianity. They will dig up verses showing the harsh judgments of God upon rebellious, sinful people, and state that (the Christian) god is not a loving god and therefore Christians cannot be a loving people. They twist the message of scripture to tout a personal agenda.

126

There will be no mention of Jesus and His sacrifice to ensure that all of us do not share a similar fate because of our sin. There will also rarely be any additional scriptural support for their view. It is typical for someone who twists scriptures to support their personal views to ignore any scripture that might state the contrary, thus illuminating their faulty context. This is usually because these people do not know the scriptures at all. Rather, they found a single verse that apparently supports their belief one way or the other.

Again, Christians – of all people – should have a problem with this. But for some reason, entire denominations seem to be quite comfortable with picking and choosing verses from scripture that support a self-serving view. Another example of such an abuse would be the following:

ACT 13:48 MKJV

(48) And hearing, the nations rejoiced and glorified the Word of the Lord. And as many as were ordained to eternal life believed.

Taking this verse only, it might be easy to come to the conclusion that those who would have eternal life will have it and that those who don't, will not, and therefore I have no need to tell anyone about the Lord. Let's face it, witnessing the Gospel is work, and it can be uncomfortable! But scripture as a whole will not support the view that fate itself is the great harvester. Jesus commissioned His followers to go into all the world and share His Gospel (Mark 16:15), a task that would hardly be necessary if our above scripture was taken in our lazy, timid, or even cowardly context. I realize that this section could easily fall under the chapter about Wrongly Dividing the Word, but what I also discovered is that many "religious" skeptics are intentionally so, because it is the coward's way. If I am skeptical that the teachings of Jesus really should apply to me, I have avoided the responsibility of acting upon those teachings. My denial of the truth makes me immune to its requirements.

STUNTED FAITH

Unfortunately, there are quite a few Christian skeptics. They are typically easy to spot because they are stunted in their faith. Beyond the most basic of doctrines about salvation and morality, they doubt everything else. They live in a form of denial. Anything beyond the sphere of what they can understand logically or what they have personally experienced presents a huge problem for them. After all, pride states that I must understand. However, God is BIG. How much of God must we demand to understand before we simply accept Him? If we demand much, then we must size Him down into parameters that we can accommodate. If we demand little, then we can have a peace that 'surpasses all understanding'.

A skeptic may see a miracle and doubt its validity, while a believing heart may see a miracle and celebrate! Yes, but what if... What if the miracle isn't from God? What if the miracle wasn't a miracle at all, but a freak of nature? What if...? Are we not to be careful? Paul warned that spiritual infants are "tossed to and fro and carried about by every wind of doctrine" (Ephesians 4:14). Jesus warned,

MAT 7:15 MKJV

(15) Beware of false prophets who come to you in sheep's clothing, but inwardly they are ravening wolves.

We must heed these warnings without becoming manic about hearing something that might lead us astray. The Holy Spirit lives in the believer in order to help him or her distinguish between Truth and everything else. Notice that Paul's admonishment was about spiritual infants. Not unlike physical babies, these should not be left alone to scavenge for spiritual food. That's what spiritual parents are for! There is a very basic filter that we can employ in order to test whether something we see or hear is of God or not: does it lead me closer to Jesus? If so, you can bet the devil had nothing to do with it!

Again, the heart of a skeptic is rooted in pride and always begins with doubt. The fundamental problem with Christian skeptics is that their god is too small and their devil is too big. They are so worried about being deceived (as perhaps Thomas was) that they fail to realize that the very Spirit that lives within them can be their guide. Scriptures show that signs and wonders follow those who believe (read about Stephen in Acts 6:8). In order to reap the most of our study of scripture, we must guard our hearts against studying from the wrong perspective.

Hunger: The
Real Key

When we think of being a Bible scholar, we think of late nights sitting at the kitchen table with the Bible open, highlighters and pencils strewn about, and a host of commentaries and dictionaries piled up. I do hope there is a little bit of that, because those can be powerful and productive times. But most of the time Bible study is not that way. It looks more like a memory verse index card stuck to the dashboard of your car. Or perhaps it's a teaching CD as you go to work. Maybe it's watching a good Bible preacher on late-night cable while trying to wind down from the day. Like so many other things in life, being a student of the Bible is something you live constantly, not something you undertake for a few hours a month. Frustration from constantly trying to learn difficult passages or memorizing scriptures (sometimes for the wrong reason) can be easily avoided by taking a few easy steps.

1. **Take it easy**. There are days when meditating on the Word of God does not mean opening the Bible. It simply means thinking about the Word that is on your heart! If you are passionate about God, that passion does not suffer if you are at the beach rather than in your study!

2. **Try to be consistent without being 'religious'.** Consistency means a constant pursuit of the things you are hungry for. If you attempt to force-feed yourself scriptures in an effort to become an expert, you are doing it for the wrong reason. Jesus scolded the Pharisees often for pursuing knowledge without pursuing a relationship. Don't do this! When traveling in my vehicle, I try to maintain a steady speed in order to arrive at my destination within a set amount of time. That doesn't mean I never speed up, slow down, or stop to rest!

3. **Understand that you cannot 'arrive' at total scriptural understanding.** The Word is deep, and rabbis who have studied scriptures for a lifetime will attest that one verse can be studied for many years and the depths of its application cannot be grasped entirely, because God's Word is a reflection of Himself. After all, would you care to worship a god who you could completely understand?

4. **Pray.** Ask God for understanding. There is much about the Word that cannot be understood without revelation from the Holy Spirit. For this revelation, we must learn to *listen*, and ask Him for guidance.

5. **Realize that some things simply will not make sense until the time is right for God to reveal the meaning.** Daniel experienced this (Dan 12:8-9). Yes, if we knew everything in scripture that we desired to know, we would probably make a big mess trying to prepare for prophetic fulfillment! Sometimes God waits until we have the character or experience necessary to handle the truths He teaches us in His word. We don't mind chopping onions in front of our small children, but we know that even though they may realize 'how' it's done, they do not yet have the experience to attempt it themselves – and God knows that onion chopping is a chore I'm ready to pass on!

In the wild, a hungry grizzly is a very dangerous animal. Why? Because a hungry animal is a brave animal – prone to go places that it normally would not venture. We must stay hungry. Hunger is truly the key to understanding scripture because it alone will prompt us to immerse ourselves in such a way as to experience Truth.

PSA 107:9 MKJV

(9) For He satisfies the thirsty soul, and fills the hungry soul with good.

Jesus also had this to say about those who are hungry:

LUK 6:21A MKJV

(21) Blessed are you who hunger now, for you shall be filled.

Spiritual hunger is a good way to determine spiritual health. Are you hungry for the things of God? If not, you may be sick! How do we stay hungry? For me, the answer is to surround myself with other hungry people. We only get more and more ravenous when we run in packs. Knowing God has a very unique effect. As my spiritual mentor explains, the more you eat, the more you hunger. Most people reading a book such as this can claim at least a modicum of spiritual hunger; a desire to learn and ingest something new. But how do we help those who have no such desire? Force feeding! Well, okay... maybe not that exactly, but if you can convince them to put some effort into a godly pursuit, they might just find out that they are slightly hungry! Get them to attend a church service with you. Get them to read a spiritual book or see a godly film. Sometimes all that's needed is a spark, right?

Oh yes, but often enough the most spiritually sick are those who are in church every week! The un-churched can be the hungriest people you will meet, while those you see in services every Sunday are about to perish from lack of spiritual nourishment. How can this be? I call this one of the traps of religion. Religion is form without substance. Religion is trying to cover oneself, usually by works or traditions, when in truth the only covering that really covers us is from God. Religion, as man has made it, is like consuming diet pills. Diet pills fool the body into thinking it is full in order to curb the appetite. The result is that nothing of substance is consumed and the mind has made peace with it. There may be reasons where this is necessary in the physical, but doing this in the spiritual is catastrophic. The devil uses man's religion to fool him into a peaceful state of malnourishment – or even terminal illness.

EAT WHILE YOU CAN!

The Bible says that there is a time coming when many will be looking for the Truth but will not be able to find it. That is a scary proposition! Spiritual famine...

AMO 8:11-12 MKJV

(11) Behold, the days come, says the Lord Jehovah, that I will send a famine in the land; not a famine of bread nor a thirst for water, but of hearing the Words of Jehovah.

(12) And they shall wander from sea to sea, and from the north even to the east; they shall run to and fro to seek the Word of Jehovah, and shall not find it.

Starving people will eat anything. Full, contented people are picky, but a starving person is not!

PRO 27:7 MKJV

(7) The full soul despises a honeycomb; but to the hungry soul every bitter thing is sweet.

That is both good and bad. The good is that when we find a starving person, they are eager to hear the good news of Jesus! The bad news is that often a starving person will gorge on the first meal they are given, and that can be poison! Cults are prospering today because they are offering attractive fare to starving people. The result is destructive. Even if a person survives such an experience, the danger is that they will no longer trust anyone and will be unwilling or unable to hear and accept the Truth. It is a good thing we serve a BIG God! This seemingly plentiful time – where "food" is everywhere – may be what Amos is referring to. People will actively search for truth, but will not find it. Why? Because the truth will be so diluted that no man will know any longer what is Truth and what is not.

I have discovered that most people are spiritually hungry even if they are not aware of it. To bring up the topic of God, His Word, or Jesus may not reveal anything but a desire to change the topic, but that does not necessarily mean they are not hungry. In fact, they may be starving! I liken it to feeding a stray cat. They are starving, yet scared to death to approach the food you are setting out. Use creativity to breach these obstacles. On a fishing trip, it is very easy to talk about creation. Even if someone does not wish to discuss inflammatory doctrines such as security of the believer, they might be willing to answer a question like, "Can you believe some people think something like this just evolved?" Oh yes, you may be opening a can of worms, but on the other hand, you're fishing, and where are they going to go (especially if they're in my boat)? When people discover you aren't judgmental of their beliefs, they tend to be more open to yours as well! Before you know it, you are inviting a starving person to a feast!

There is a popular beer commercial on television that I see from time to time. It's for Dos Equis Beer. Their little buzz-line is "Stay Thirsty, my Friends". It's hardly profound, for what it is. But on the other hand... the Christian community should adopt such a motto. We must stay hungry for the Word. We must stay thirsty for the Spirit. There's this tension again that we must deal with.

JOH 6:35 MKJV

(35) And Jesus said to them, I am the bread of life. He who comes to Me shall never hunger, and he who believes on Me shall never thirst.

What is the object – to be hungry or to be satiated? If we go to the Greek, we see that the meaning of 'hungry' is 'to be famished'. We should never be in a spot where we are starving from lack, but we should always be in a place where eating is an inviting prospect!

When I go on vacations, the main reason I go is to eat out. My dad is the same way. My mom, on the other hand – not so much. Dad and I go first to eat, and secondly to see the sights or whatever else. We can walk out of a restaurant, look at each other, and say, "What sounds good for dinner?" Or no matter where we are or what time of day it is, if one of us asks the other if they are hungry, the answer is usually, "I could eat!" This is the way I am with the Word. I can always consume. There is never a time when it does not sound good! I stay hungry. The reason is similar to my restaurant experiences. I cannot promise you that every time I have delved into the Word I have come away satisfied, or even glad I did. After all, the Word can convict and scold. But there were far more times I went with little expectation and got blown away by what I learned or experienced in my spirit. These only make the spirit hungrier.

INVITE QUESTIONS

When you are hungry, it isn't always easy to find just what you are hungry for. Have you ever just stared at the open refrigerator? It's frustrating, isn't it! Perhaps the greatest boon to my learning the Word has been when others ask me questions. When I am in an environment of questions, my heart starts to race. Why? Because questions come from every which way the wind blows. You get every perspective when people ask questions. Questions reveal so much to me! Most of the time, I am in awe of the one who asks. How on earth would a person come up with such a brilliant thought? Who would have thought to ask THAT? I have lost count of the number of times I was asked a question that prompted tremendous spiritual discovery in my own life. Often times, I know the general vicinity in which a treasure may be buried, but lack the precise location. A good question will reveal that to me. Many of the nuggets I have already spoken of in this book came to me first in the form of a question from someone who desired to know. Had they never asked...? I never would have picked up the shovel!

If you are new to studying the Word, and you simply have no place to start, encourage someone you know to ask you some questions. It can be your five year old, or your wife, or your dad. Start the conversation with, "What are some things about the Bible that you have always wanted to know, but never found an answer to?" The question you are looking for is NOT the one for which you already know the answer. You are looking for the head-scratcher. Try this story on for size. I want to present it from the King James Version:

JDG 11:30-40 KJV

(30) And Jephthah vowed a vow unto the LORD, and said, If thou shalt without fail deliver the children of Ammon into mine hands,

(31) Then it shall be, that whatsoever cometh forth of the doors of my house to meet me, when I return in peace from the children of Ammon, shall surely be the LORD'S, and I will offer it up for a burnt offering.

(32) So Jephthah passed over unto the children of Ammon to fight against them; and the LORD delivered them into his hands.

(33) And he smote them from Aroer, even till thou come to Minnith, even twenty cities, and unto the plain of the vineyards, with a very great slaughter. Thus the children of Ammon were subdued before the children of Israel.

(34) And Jephthah came to Mizpeh unto his house, and, behold, his daughter came out to meet him with timbrels and with dances: and she was his only child; beside her he had neither son nor daughter.

(35) And it came to pass, when he saw her, that he rent his clothes, and said, Alas, my daughter! thou hast brought me very low, and thou art one of them that trouble me: for I have opened my mouth unto the LORD, and I cannot go back.

(36) And she said unto him, My father, if thou hast opened thy mouth unto the LORD, do to me according to that which hath proceeded out of thy mouth; forasmuch as the LORD hath taken vengeance for thee of thine enemies, even of the children of Ammon.

(37) And she said unto her father, Let this thing be done for me: let me alone two months, that I may go up and down upon the mountains, and bewail my virginity, I and my fellows.

(38) And he said, Go. And he sent her away for two months: and she went with her companions, and bewailed her virginity upon the mountains.

(39) And it came to pass at the end of two months, that she returned unto her father, who did with her according to his vow which he had vowed: and she knew no man. And it was a custom in Israel,

(40) That the daughters of Israel went yearly to lament the daughter of Jephthah the Gileadite four days in a year.

If that story doesn't raise questions in your mind, you are much more enlightened than me! My first question is, "What in the world just happened?" Let's ask some more.

- Didn't Jephthah know that might be a dangerous thing to vow?
- Did God inspire that vow at all?
- Why would God even honor such a vow?

- Did Jephthah really burn up his daughter as a sacrifice?
- Why would Jephthah's daughter be worried about her virginity, of all things?
- Why, oh why, is the outcome of this story not made clear? Does God not care about the conclusion we are left with?

Yes, my mind was a whirlwind of these questions after reading the story. Now how in the world (another question) does one get to the bottom of this? The reason I went with the King James is that it presented the story in a very raw form. Basically, the King James took a literal approach to translating the phrase, "offer it up for a burnt offering." The MKJV as well as several other translations used the dynamic equivalency method and came up with "offer it up *instead* of a burnt offering." The italicized word 'instead' was added because the translator refused to believe that Jephthah actually sacrificed his daughter. Do you see how the translator can take liberty? Does this mean the translator was incorrect? No, it doesn't, but it does mean that the translator made a decision in this case that possibly influences our conclusion. Let's go back to our questions. Did Jephthah have no clue that his daughter might come out of the house? I don't know – maybe she was supposed to be staying with the folks. Or maybe he was used to seeing farm animals bolting about whenever he approached his homestead. This would make more sense, right? Not really. Nothing really makes sense here, still. What did God have to do with this vow?

JDG 10:15-18 MKJV

(15)   And the sons of Israel said to Jehovah, We have sinned. Do You to us whatever is good in Your eyes; only deliver us, we pray You, today.

(16)   And they put away the strange gods from among them, and served Jehovah. And His soul was moved by the misery of Israel.

(17) Then the sons of Ammon were gathered and camped in Gilead. And the sons of Israel assembled themselves together and camped in Mizpeh.

(18) And the people and rulers of Gilead said to one another, What man is there who will begin to fight against the sons of Ammon? He shall be head over all the inhabitants of Gilead.

Taken from the previous chapter, we see here that God had already determined to free His repentant people. It was a done deal – it was GOING to happen. When Jephthah stepped into this role, his success was guaranteed. Why, then, did Jephthah see fit to bargain with God for an outcome that was already set? Regardless of all other conclusions we might draw, we can learn a lot from that right there! Knowing that the conclusion was foregone – God intended to save Israel from Ammon – is there any way that we can say that God came into agreement with Jephthah's foolish vow? That brings us down to whether or not Jephthah really did what scriptures hint at. At this point, let's take a look at some historical facts. For a thank offering such as Noah's after the flood, the offering was always a male. It was a male lamb or goat offered upon the bronze altar in the desert by the Levites. It was always a bull, never a cow. Abraham offered Isaac. God offered Jesus. Secondly, there was never a time outside of Isaac when God asked for or otherwise required a human sacrifice. This was part of the blessing that Abraham bestowed upon all of humanity. His willingness to offer Isaac prompted God to offer His own Son instead, removing the need forever for a human sacrifice to satisfy a requirement of God. As well, Jephthah would have had to kill his own daughter, as no priest would have been willing to do so, even to satisfy a vow of another. Why then did Jephthah's nameless daughter ask to mourn her virginity for two months? Most likely, this was because she was to be dedicated to temple service for the rest of her life, forfeiting a normal life of marriage and childbearing. Being Jephthah's only offspring, the inheritance he left would also go to someone else. In that culture, tragic, for him!

You could call this a large obstacle to the non-death outcome of this story, but why might the other daughters of Israel lament Jephthah's daughter four times a year if she was not sacrificed? Strangely enough, the word 'lament' there also means 'to celebrate or commemorate'. Strong's concordance tells me that much. When I do a search on that Strong's number (H8567) I discover that the word is only used one other time in scripture:

JDG 5:11 MKJV

(11) Louder than the voice of the dividers between the watering places, there shall they tell again the righteous acts of Jehovah, the righteous acts of His leaders in Israel. Then shall the people of Jehovah go down to the gates.

It means "tell again", just as one might re-enact a story of a hero by play or by skit. Great stuff! So what does it all mean? Did Jephthah or did he not sacrifice his daughter by killing her? Judging by the Law under which Jephthah lived, I would say he did not, but ultimately God chose to be vague here. Why might He do this? I believe that what we do not know is truly as important as what we do know.

- God does not require a sacrifice of death from us any longer. He wants us to be a living sacrifice (Romans 12:1).
- There was a time when more than anything else, the world needed a perfect sacrifice - a Savior.
- God did require a man to follow through with his vow (Ecclesiastes 5:4-5).
- Singular vows were perfectly acceptable to God. A man could devote himself, his children, his servants, his cattle, or his goods for sacred service in the sanctuary (Leviticus 27).
- Jephthah, like Abraham, was willing to give up his only offspring because of his vow.

HOW DEEP CAN I GO?

So now that we have seen some methods of study and we have seen some mysteries in the scripture revealed, we might ask, just how far does all this go? Yes, I see how passages can have different meanings and maybe even how they can have different layers of meaning, but is this what it all boils down to? Let me share another example that shows more depth than we have seen to this point. It's fairly simple.

In the book of Exodus, we read the story of how God redeemed His people from under the yoke of slavery. Unfortunately, they had a desert to cross before they could enter the land that was promised to them. As a result, the people grumbled constantly.

NUM 21:5-6 MKJV

(5) And the people spoke against God and against Moses, Why have you brought us up out of Egypt to die in the wilderness? For there is no bread, neither is there any water. And our soul hates this light bread.

(6) And Jehovah sent fiery serpents among the people, and they bit the people. And many people of Israel died.

Talk about making a bad situation worse! These folks were really in trouble! Not unlike our own children, the minute they discovered the scope of their predicament they were immediately sorry. Moses interceded for them, and God gave him a solution.

NUM 21:7-8 MKJV

(7) And the people came to Moses and said, We have sinned, for we have spoken against Jehovah and against you. Pray to Jehovah that He take away the serpents from us. And Moses prayed for the people.

(8) And Jehovah said to Moses, Make a fiery serpent and set it on a pole. And it shall be when everyone that is bitten, when he looks upon it, he shall live.

It seems a little nonsensical, doesn't it? Maybe not if we view this through a spiritual lens. Let's ask some questions. What was the problem the people had? Snakes! God's response was to cast a representation of the problem, lift it up, and have anyone who would to look upon that as the solution and they would be saved. That's different, isn't it! Notice, it never says that when the people would look upon the serpent, their wounds would quit hurting – simply that they would live.

To a sinful world, according to God and His scriptures, we have the same issue. Sin is killing us. The wages of sin are death (Rom 6:23). What is God going to do about it? As you might guess, His solution is the same. Take our sin, put it on a pole, and lift it up in order to redeem us. It doesn't mean that sin will cease to hurt while we live this mortal life, but it does mean we will live – forever! I realize that for some, this is a head-scratcher because I am obviously comparing the snake on the pole to Jesus on the cross, and it seems like a very bad choice for comparison. Scripture says, however, that Jesus became sin for us (2 Corinthians 5:21) so that we might be redeemed.

REDEMPTION COSTS

Again, this redemption has always been a big deal to God. He wished us to know from the beginning that redemption costs something. When He brought the children of Israel out of Egypt, He had Moses count the people and pay half a shekel of silver (silver represents redemption) for each man that came out of Egypt.

EXO 30:12 MKJV

> (12) When you count the sons of Israel, of those who are to be counted, then they shall each man give a ransom for his soul to Jehovah when you number them, so that there may be no plague among them when you number them.

Moses did this! But quite a few years later, David also num-
bered the people of Israel, but guess what he did not do? He did
not pay the ransom price for all of the known redeemed.

2SA 24:15 MKJV

(15) And Jehovah sent a plague upon Israel from the
morning even till the time appointed. And there died
from the people, from Dan to Beer-sheba, seventy thousand men.

This would certainly be a usable example in several other chapters on fueling worldly arguments pertaining to the goodness of
God. The point of it all is this: Redemption is not, nor has it
ever been free. There is a price for it. God paid that price for
us, through Jesus. He then offered it to us free of charge, but we
should understand that He paid dearly for it. So how deep can we
go?

DEU 15:15 MKJV

(15) And you shall remember that you were a slave in
the land of Egypt, and Jehovah your God redeemed you.
Therefore I command you this thing today.

The word "redeem" here is the Hebrew word 'ga-al'. In Modern
Hebrew it would look like: , read from right to left – gimmel,
aleph, lamed. Removing the gimmel (the first letter on the right),
we have the spelling of the word for God (aleph, lamed). In ancient
Hebrew, each letter has a meaning that is significant. In this case,
gimmel is a symbol that resembles a backwards "L", and it means
'pride', or 'lifting up'. Pride is the process of lifting ourselves up.
But in the ancient pictograph form of Hebrew, we take this gimmel and add it on to our word for 'God' to create our word 'ga-al',
or 'redeem', and we see that redemption is God being Lifted Up.
The most ancient form of the language also tells the gospel story!
How deep would you like to go?

144

THE QUESTION SECTION

Several times in this book I have touched upon the value of asking questions. The question is the display of hunger. The question is useful for introspection as well, which is why it was a favored tool of the rabbis. Here are some questions I have asked in the past. The Lord has revealed to me the answers to some of these. This section might give you some insight to how analytical my mind is. Some questions may seem silly, if you analyze questions, but at the same time I think they may be relevant. I wish to provoke you to seek answers. I wish to pique your curiosity. It's that simple.

- What is God's plan to reach people who have never heard of Jesus?
- What happens to those people when they die?
- Who were the giants, and why would God allow such beings to corrupt His creation?
- Could animals talk in the Garden of Eden, or is it just that Adam could understand them?
- When did the dinosaurs live?
- Did God create dangerous and annoying things like mosquitoes, or did the devil play a part in that?
- Why does it seem as though some animals were intrinsically designed for eating meat, and yet we are told in Genesis that they only ate vegetation and seeds?
- Were all of those rules really necessary for the children of Israel to follow? Was it a matter of survival?
- Can't we ignore the Old Testament? Isn't it irrelevant?
- Is God finished creating?
- What is the Tribulation Period and will I have to go through that?
- Were the Pharisees all bad people?
- Why did God allow all those bad things to happen to Job?
- If it is appointed for man once to die, then why do so many believe that they will be raptured?
- Does the Bible speak of a rapture event?
- Will those who return with Jesus at Armageddon be allowed to fight?

- If the covenant of the Old Testament was replaced by an improved and perfect covenant (Hebrews 9) then why does it seems like God's people were so much more powerful back then?
- Why is there such a difference between Old Testament prophets and New Testament prophets?
- Who was Melchizedek and what was his significance?
- Why did Jonathan shoot arrows past his servant as a signal to David that his father was trying to kill him, and then run out and meet him in the field? Could he not have simply relayed the message personally?
- Why is the universe so incredibly, immeasurably vast?
- Are we the only living beings in the created universe?
- If the universe is expanding, what does that imply about the character of God?
- How could a man like Judas Iscariot live, walk, eat, and breathe with Jesus daily and not truly believe He was who He said He was?
- If baptism is so important, what effect did not being baptized have on the thief on the cross?
- Is God's will always done?
- Does God laugh?
- Are dates significant to God?
- Isn't the book of Revelation mostly symbolic?
- How do we know what is symbolic and what is not?
- Do good people go to hell?
- Why do bad things happen to good people?

WAXING
ELOQUENT

Now that we have come to the end of this book on studying the Bible, I would like to say this. The last thing the world needs is another Bible study. The Bible is God's word. I believe it is divinely inspired and profitable for teaching and edification and all of that good stuff, just as it claims. Unfortunately, memorizing every word of scripture will not bring you one step closer to God - without faith. The Pharisees were experts on the written word of their day – the Torah and the prophets and the poetic books. Many of them had it all memorized. For all of that, they could not recognize Jesus when He came to them. A head-knowledge of Jesus never saved anyone. Scripture says that we are all called. Judas Iscariot was called by Christ – chosen, to be more accurate. He responded in the physical, but I believe he never responded in his spirit. So who did respond to Jesus? The tax collectors did. The prostitutes did. The fishermen, the tent makers, the diseased and broken, and the children all saw Him for who He was. What was the difference between those who recognized Him and those who didn't? For many, the difference was "Bible studies". The knowledge they possessed made them prideful in their own hearts to the point where their own preconceived ideas about Messiah became their downfall.

It is my hope that any tips or revelation you may have received from this book will serve to draw you closer to the author of the Bible. I desire to show everyone that the scriptures are so incredibly crafted that they could not possibly be the handiwork of any man. If we can get that in our head and heart, then we can begin to accept what it says as what it means. Picking and choosing our own personal truths out of scripture is illegal. Intellectually, our head may allow us to get by with that for a season, but our spirit knows we are lying to ourselves. Additionally, the very act of reading the Bible changes things. Like those who stood and listened to Jesus teach, reading the Word forces me to make a decision, either consciously or not. Do I accept what I am reading as truth? Do I not? In this regard, the Bible is a dangerous book to read. If the words in it are true, then we will all be held accountable for each word we read, digest, and follow. In the Lord of the Rings Trilogy by J.R.R. Tolkien, there is a dialogue between King Theoden of Rohan and Aragorn.

KING THEODEN: I know what it is you want of me but I will not bring further death to my people. I will not risk open war.
ARAGORN: Open war is upon you, whether you would risk it or not!

That resonates because we are ALL at war. While this war may not be of our choosing, it is upon us whether we choose to fight it or not. If you choose not to fight, he wins. The ostrich is a bird that has a reputation of hiding its head in the sand if afraid. Although this behavior is likely mythical, the idea of "out of sight, out of mind" is very popular to people. We don't like to think of bankruptcy, so we don't prepare financially. We don't like thinking of heart problems, so we don't eat right. We don't like thinking of death, so we don't prepare a will. Many take this approach to studying scripture. They don't like thinking of death, or judgment, or the end of the age because let's face it – we are afraid of the unknown and much of what the Bible says is scary. Ignorance is bliss, yes? For a while this may be.

GEN 20:2-6 MKJV

(2) And Abraham said of Sarah his wife, She is my sister. And Abimelech the king of Gerar sent and took Sarah.

(3) But God came to Abimelech in a dream by night, and said to him, Behold, you are about to die, for the woman whom you have taken; for she is a man's wife.

(4) But Abimelech had not come near her. And he said, Lord, will You also kill a righteous nation?

(5) Did he not say to me, She is my sister? And she, even she herself said, He is my brother. In the sincerity of my heart and innocency of my hands I have done this.

(6) And God said to him in a dream, Yes, I know that you did this in the sincerity of your heart. For I also withheld you from sinning against Me. Therefore I did not allow you to touch her.

Do you know what this story reveals? Ignorance is no excuse! Such is the character of God to have mercy upon us when things happen beyond our control. He showed this to Abimelech. Yet, for most of us, reading the scriptures and accepting them for the truths found within are well within our abilities and options. We have the Word. Do we read it? Do we take it to heart? Or do we bury our heads in the sand because we are afraid that the Light of Truth will reveal the darkness in our own lives? This fear is something we all must come to terms with.

COPYRIGHT INFORMATION

DEDICATION

I *would like to dedicate this book to my twin daughters, Eliza and Malakya.*
They have taught me more about the Majesty of God in a short time than
I have learned in a lifetime. May my ceiling be your floor! Thank you to
my wife, Darci, who never let life spiral out of control while I was "busy".
Thank you to my Dad and Mom who laid a solid biblical foundation for
me – and still do. Also, thank you, Stan, for being a Father to all of us
and setting the bar high!

Made in the USA
Charleston, SC
23 July 2012